Richard Shears was born in I
in Australia with his wife I
winning foreign correspondent for the *Daily Mail* and
is also the author of 30 books, many of them focused
on true crime. His work as a journalist has taken him
to wars in Ireland, East Timor, Afghanistan and Iraq.

His books include *Swamp*, an investigation into the
death of once-wealthy spinster Margaret Clement,
Wildlife Warrior, on the life and death of Australian
Steve Irwin and *Bloodstain*, the vanishing and presumed
murder of British backpacker Peter Falconio in the
Australian outback.

THE GIGOLO, THE HEIRESS AND THE BLACKMAIL PLOT

RICHARD SHEARS

NEW HOLLAND

CONTENTS

PART FOUR: THE PLOT UNRAVELS

Published in 2009 by New Holland Publishers (UK) Ltd
London • Cape Town • Sydney • Auckland
www.newhollandpublishers.com
Garfield House, 86–88 Edgware Road, London W2 2EA, United Kingdom
80 McKenzie Street, Cape Town 8001, South Africa
Unit 1, 66 Gibbes Street, Chatswood, NSW 2067, Australia
218 Lake Road, Northcote, Auckland, New Zealand

10 9 8 7 6 5 4 3 2 1

A catalogue record for this book is available from the British Library

ISBN 978 1 84773 633 8

Publishing Director: Rosemary Wilkinson
Publisher: Aruna Vasudevan
Project Editor: Julia Shone
Copy-editor: Scala Quin
Design Manager: Phil Kay
Book Design: Rebecca Longworth
Cover Design: Hello Paul Ltd
Production: Melanie Dowland
DTP: Tammy Warren

Reproduction by Pica Digital PTE Ltd, Singapore
Printed and bound by Athenaeum Press Ltd, Gateshead, UK

PROLOGUE

Zurich was overhung with blue and bathed in winter sunshine as the dark green diesel Mercedes S 300 left the tourists behind on Monday 14 January 2008, and took the E70 towards Winterthur, his old stamping ground. He checked the mirror, making sure that the Audi off-roader was still behind him. After today's rendezvous, he might treat himself to a better vehicle – over 10 years old, his Merc was getting a bit long in the tooth.

Helg Sgarbi was feeling on top of the world and, in reality, he soon would be. Up ahead, to the north-east, among the mountain ranges, he'd be collecting a cool 14 million euros, *in hard cash*.

The woman would pay up. She had no choice. Anyone in her position would … there was no way she would allow any scandal to touch her or her family. Nor would she want the whole Nazi thing brought up again.

He let his thoughts drift … Was *that* it? Was all this just revenge for what her grandfather had done to his family decades before in the war? He would have to let others be the judge of that because the man in the car behind him, to whom he had told everything, would certainly talk if he had to – if it all went wrong. *But it wouldn't.* No chance of that. She simply had too much to lose.

Soon, he was leading Ernani Barretta through Winterthur, or 'Winti' as the locals called it, a place where he'd been at school some 40 years previously. The town had stood pretty much on its own in those days when he had attended secondary and then high school, but today it was a satellite town of Zurich. He would never have dreamed, as he ran through the streets of the old town with his school friends, all those years ago, that so much wealth would come his way.

He checked the mirror. Ernani was still right behind him in the Audi. His focus swung back to his own face – the light brown hair, the square jaw and, behind the designer spectacles, the blue–grey eyes that had captured the hearts of so many women. What was it the Comtesse had called him? *Her own personal James Bond!* And, that other wealthy executive he'd seduced, she'd called him that as well – even her children had started asking her about '007'.

There had been so many compliments from so many others in so many places – Munich, Zurich, Rome, Monte Carlo – that he could barely hold back a chuckle even now. What had he been called? *'Suave'*, *'sophisticated'*, *'a perfect gentleman'*, a *'Clark Kent look-alike'*, *'greatest of lovers'*, *'Superman'*, *'secret agent'*, *'Indiana Jones'* – the list was endless: he was a hero to them all.

They had come from all walks of life – or rather, from every section of the upper echelons of European society – those rich, lonely women, who craved his company. If they didn't have a few million euros tucked away in their bank accounts, they really weren't worth getting into bed with. The sex, putting aside the ancient Comtesse, of course, was one thing; but it was the money that was the ultimate prize.

Soon, the two cars were leaving Switzerland behind and crossing the border into Austria. The sky was turning grey and as they headed towards Innsbruck, the landscape turned white with fallen snow.

He had arranged the place for their rendezvous. In Germany, she had always been careful not to be seen in public with him, although to any onlooker they might have passed as a successful businessman and his elegant wife. Of course, he could understand why she should continue to exercise caution, especially since he had tightened the noose.

Close to the mountains, where they were now to meet, was an area that they both knew well. Perhaps she would feel more comfortable in these familiar surroundings. But her emotions were of no concern to him really. Whatever feelings she had had for him – infatuation, love, curiosity – and he believed they were real – didn't matter now as he certainly wouldn't have to fake his own emotions any more. The handover of cash would be brief. There would be no loving embrace from her this time, he felt sure.

Behind him, Barretta flashed his lights and Sgarbi let him pass. The Italian in his gleaming new white, four-wheel drive was probably fed up with following the old Merc, but if he wanted to test his own car's grip on the icy roads he would be disappointed. The highway was particularly busy with travellers heading up to the mountain resorts in the Tyrol for their winter downhill- and cross-country-skiing vacations, and the amount of traffic was keeping the surface fairly ice-free.

The snow lay thick on the surrounding mountains. It was going to be bitterly cold in the rest stop, which was notorious anyway for catching the wintry gusts. The shifting of the money from her car to his would have to be quick or they'd all freeze to death!

As they passed the turn-off to Innsbruck, he could not help stealing a glance towards the mountains to the South. Up there was a world that few people could imagine, but which he knew well – the Lanserhof spa and health centre, boasting holistic treatments of the future. Not your average pick-up joint, he had joked with Ernani, when he'd planned it, but she was no average woman and he certainly didn't consider himself an *average* man. His many wealthy conquests were testament to that – and there had been none greater than the winning of the heart of the woman he was due to meet and whose millions he would possess more of before the day was out.

How *well* he had read her. He'd dipped his toe in the water, so to speak, tested her reaction to his softly–softly approach and within a few minutes of talking with her he knew that he'd be able to hook her. His homework had been invaluable. The woman hadn't even told her future husband who she was until she was certain that he truly loved her. So, when he, Helg Sgarbi, set out to win her, he gave the impression that he had no idea who she was.

The scene that day at the Lanserhof came back to him as if it were yesterday. She had been lying back in the sun reading a book, the water from a small pond trickling nearby. Of course, he'd researched the book himself that she was reading, and he knew the storyline almost as well as the author did! Casually, he'd dropped into conversation the names of a couple of key characters, made mention of the spiritual element behind the plot and gradually he could see that the barriers that she'd worked so hard to build up over a lifetime were beginning to crumble. There had still been a lot of work to do but he'd opened a crack in her defences. Something as simple as being able to discuss a book had allowed him to penetrate the mind of one of the world's most secretive women. Not to mention one of the wealthiest.

He turned his attention back to the road in front of him. Not so far now. He'd made the meeting point easy for her. A drive of about 150km (93 miles) south from Munich for the woman, whereas his own journey was some 100km (62 miles) more. She knew this area well though: the autobahn cut through mountain valleys through which they'd strolled together during the days of relaxation spent at the Lanserhof, weeks before their romance had even started. If truth be told, he'd actually enjoyed those walks and the fresh mountain air.

The signpost ahead announced 'Vomp', a small town 563m up into the mountains with a population of just over 4,300. More heavy snows were forecast there – such a contrast to the lush and green vales that had filled the eye when he'd first begun his seduction of the woman in that summery July, six months earlier.

To the North lay the Karwendelgebirge, the mountain range that separated Austria from Bavaria in southern Germany. That was her territory. Her territory in more ways than one – if her powerful company, her luxury home and her enormous wealth counted.

She'd be on her way to the meeting point, perhaps in her favourite little car, the Mini. But it was possible, for the sake of concealing her movements and because of the space needed for the two huge boxes of money that she was required to bring with her, she'd be in a company car. *Company* car. *Her company, literally.* What she'd have told her husband as an excuse for her absence was her problem. She'd be able to make it back to Munich by the end of the day, in any case. He knew that her husband, Jan, had suspected that she was having an affair in the past – that much she had told him. That was too bad. For himself, none of this was about love. It never had been. The money, his family perhaps – the money, certainly.

Ernani's right indicator flicked on. The Italian was turning into the Rosenberger rest stop, the rendezvous-point, where he, Helg Sgarbi, perhaps the world's most successful gigolo, would collect the biggest pay-off of his life. Others who craved the money of wealthy women had had to endure the tie of marriage and years of subservience, but not him. Time and again he'd proved that a few silken words had much more power than a wedding ring on women.

He was exultant. Not long now. The embarrassment, the scandal, which would erupt if she didn't turn up, was too great a risk for her to take. Hadn't he already sent her a sample of that sex video? If that got out … *No*, he'd read her too well; he was absolutely confident that she wouldn't take any chances where her privacy, which had always been watertight, was concerned. It was unthinkable for her to consider backing out of this essential 'business deal', no matter how long she might have agonized over it.

He pulled into a parking space away from the main building. Ernani found another spot close by. The cafeteria was bustling. It was a popular rest stop and had an enticing note on its website declaring: '*We warmly welcome you and wish you a pleasant stay.*'

More vehicles pulled in behind them. If he'd only taken more notice of those cars on the autobahn instead of keeping his eyes on Ernani's Audi, things might have turned out differently. If he'd only been less engrossed in his own thoughts and 'achievements', he might have sensed that all was not as it should have been and he might not have been so shocked at what happened next.

The tourists visiting the skiing regions of the Tyrol were actually members of Cobra, Austria's crack anti-terrorist squad. Regarded as one of the most efficient units in the world, Cobra, headed by Hannes Gülnbrein, is called in to resolve hostage situations when negotiations fail, protect people regarded as being at high risk, provide security escorts for large sums of money and arrest dangerous criminals, among other things.

The police in Switzerland had obtained an international warrant for the men's arrest and Cobra, cooperating with them, had followed the two cars along the autobahn to a rendezvous-point of which they were already aware. Helg was actually checking his watch when the door of his Merc was suddenly thrown open and a Glock–17 9mm pistol was pointed at his face. There were men in balaclavas and dark khaki uniforms also levelling Steyr assault rifles at him. Across the parking lot, he could see more armed men surrounding Barretta's Audi. The game was up, it seemed. *It was utterly unbelievable.*

Even as he climbed slowly from his faithful old Merc and raised his hands in the air, he couldn't help but smile – a smile which was, in the following months, to become one of the most widely recognized in Europe.

So ... she'd actually done it! She'd gone to the authorities. Pulled off a reverse sting. He'd never thought for a moment that one of the richest women in Europe – certainly the most affluent in Germany, and the 55th wealthiest person in the world – would ever be so courageous. He hadn't thought she'd had it in her.

Even as they marched him away at gunpoint to a police car he knew that this whole business would eventually leak out to the press and that the woman's identity, the affair, the blackmail, everything would be on everyone's lips around the world. How could it not?

Her name was Susanne Klatten and she was the head of *Bayerische Moteren Werke* (Bavarian Motor Works) or BMW, as it is more commonly known – the iconic international manufacturer of luxury cars. One of the most powerful and influential women in the world, Susanne was worth a cool 10 billion euros. And, a small slice of that, a very small part of that fortune had just slipped right through Helg Sgarbi's fingers.

PART ONE
Susanne

A DANGEROUS ERA

The family motto could well have been a single word: *Wachsamkeit* – 'vigilance'. For most of her life she had made that her mantra, stepping out into the world with caution. But sometimes rules are made to be broken – sometimes deliberately, sometimes accidentally. Often, such edicts are just too difficult to follow, particularly as the decades pass by and a rule becomes a wall or a prison, smothering any cry for release.

Susanne Klatten, née Quandt, was born on 28 April 1962. Astrologers would say that looking at the privileges that she has since enjoyed, no star sign could better suit her than that of Taurus. Those born under the sign of the Bull are said to revel in material goods, get their kicks from the rewards of any challenge, while also taking delight in a tender, sensual touch. But astrologers look at the abstract, whereas Susanne, on the other hand, had to deal with the harsh realities of her life and wealth – the constant and dangerous threat to her life that existed simply because of who she was and the family into which she had been born.

She was surrounded by great and undeniable wealth from the moment that she came into the world, but that, along with a Nazi-associated family history, which would haunt her and would also go some way to explaining why she would keep such a private and very low profile, were both to become her own personal curse.

Wealth, whether acquired through the accident of birth or through personal success, often breeds envy and greed. Those who do not have it, may resort to all kinds of methods, some rather extreme, to acquire it, including robbery, deception, blackmail, extortion, kidnapping and, in worst-case scenarios, murder. Many rich and famous people live in constant fear of a violent intrusion into their lives and sometimes, whatever the measures they might take to protect themselves and their families, evil can find a way in.

The sons and daughters of the rich and famous are often the most at risk. To take a well-known but horrific example, in 1932 Charles A. Lindbergh, Jr, the 20-month-old son of the American aviator Charles Lindbergh and his wife, Anne, was abducted from the family home in New Jersey. After a series of ransom notes, a payment of US $50,000 was handed over to a stranger – but the baby was never returned. He had been dead for more than two months, his skull crushed by a blow to the head.

Another example is that of John Paul Getty, III, more commonly known as 'Paul', the 16-year-old grandson of American industrialist Jean Paul Getty, once named by *Fortune* magazine as the richest living American. Paul was kidnapped in July 1973, whilst living in Rome. A phone demand was made for US $17 million and later a lock of hair and a human ear alleged to be the boy's was delivered to his family, along with a note saying that if the money wasn't paid he would 'arrive in little bits'.

Eventually, Paul was returned after his grandfather brokered a deal to hand over US $2 million to the kidnappers. They, in turn, were never captured. The effect on Paul was devastating. The trauma turned him to drugs, to which he became addicted and, by 1981, the dope and alcohol had robbed him of his powers of speech and left him paralysed and blind.

Paul's kidnapping was just one of a blight of similar crimes that plagued southern Europe, Italy in particular, in the 1970s and 80s. The children of several wealthy families were snatched from the streets and many victims were never seen again. The worst year was 1975, when more than 80 people, many of them children, were held to ransom. The police managed to stem the flow of kidnappings by freezing the bank accounts of targeted families, but this made it impossible, or at least extremely difficult, for them to pay up, even had they wanted to. Hardly a year passed without a ransom demand, although many of the cases remained secret, for it was in the interest of everyone involved to keep quiet about the fact that money was being exchanged with criminals to safeguard the return of their loved ones.

Germany initially appeared to have escaped the worst of the kidnapping plots and it seemed quite safe for Susanne and her younger brother, Stefan, to walk the few hundred metres from their home in Bad Homburg, near Frankfurt, to the Kaiserin–Friedrich–Gymnasium, one of the oldest schools in the country. But despite the peaceful surroundings that the wealthy residents of Bad Homburg enjoyed, Germans had no cause to be complacent at that time. The seeds of a new and terrifying era had already been sewn and the consequences of it were about to be felt – not just in the big cities, but also in Bad Homburg itself.

In 1967, when Susanne was just five years old, police killed a young activist in Berlin during a demonstration against a visit by the US-backed Shah of Iran. A left-wing student, Andreas Baader, concluded that the authorities that had risen to power in the years since 1945, the end of the Second World War, were no better than the Nazis themselves. In 1968, Baader hit back by detonating home-made bombs in two Frankfurt department stores, just 20km (12 miles) from the Bad Homburg villa where the young Susanne Quandt was living. He was subsequently arrested and sent to prison, but escaped two years later with the help of a left-wing journalist, Ulrike Meinhof. They formed the Red Army Faction (RAF), more popularly known as the Baader–Meinhof gang, a group that was to bring fear into the hearts and homes of every German at that time.

Several RAF members made their way to Jordan, where they learned how to use AK–47 (Kalashnikov) rifles at a camp run by the Palestinian Liberation Organization (PLO). With their newly acquired skills, the gang spent the next two years robbing banks and bombing buildings around Germany. Eventually in early June 1972, Baader was recaptured, this time with accomplices Jan-Carl Raspe and Holger Meins, during a shootout in Frankfurt. Two weeks later, Meinhof was also taken prisoner.

But if Germans believed that was the end of the gang's activities, they were to be sadly mistaken, for a new generation of militants was already planning a further series of attacks against the right-wing authorities – in particular targeting anyone wealthy, and previously associated with the Hitler regime. The Quandt family ticked all the boxes to become RAF kidnap, or worse murder targets.

In 1975, the German Embassy in Stockholm was attacked by the RAF, who took 11 people hostage, including the Ambassador. They demanded the release of 26 RAF 'political prisoners', held in Germany. The siege, which lasted 12 hours, resulted in the deaths of two attachés. The trial of the 26 Baader–Meinhof members began in 1976 and lasted almost two years. Meinhof allegedly hanged herself with towels in her cell, an event that led to a new wave of terror and political assassinations in 1977.

The chief public prosecutor in the trial of other gang members was killed in Karlsruhe by a hitman on a motor cycle in April of that year and in July the chief executive of the Dresden Bank, Jürgen Ponto, was shot dead in front of his home in Oberursel, only 4.8km (3 miles) from the Quandt home. He was not only a friend of the Quandts but Susanne Albrecht, one of the leading members of the RAF and one of the people who killed him, was his god daughter – a fact that brought home that absolutely no-one could be trusted when money or politics were at stake. That shocking crime was just too close to the Quandt villa for comfort: protection around the family was subsequently increased.

Then matters became worse for the Quandts – and every other family with connections to the Nazi regime. On 5 September 1977, Hanns-Martin Schleyer, one of Germany's most powerful industrialists, and the man who had commented at Ponto's memorial service that the next Baader–Meinhof victim was certainly present, was being chauffeured in his Mercedes through the streets of Cologne, when a woman with a pushchair stepped out in front of his car. The driver was forced to brake. At the same time, a car reversed into the Mercedes. Schleyer's driver and the three police officers with him had absolutely no time to react when the woman pulled out two machine guns from the pushchair. In a hail of bullets everyone but Schleyer was killed by the woman and her accomplices. Schleyer was dragged from the car and driven off. Then came the demand – the German government had to release imprisoned members of the Baader–Meinhof gang.

Schleyer's kidnapping was of considerable concern to the 15-year-old Susanne's family, for, like the industrialist, not only were they extremely wealthy, but they also had connections to the Nazi war machine. Whereas Schleyer had been a mid-ranking SS officer in the Third Reich, and had been a member in his younger days of Hitler Youth, the Quandt family's background reached back not just to Hitler but to his leading commandants as well, Goebbels among them, and also, perhaps more shockingly, to the concentration camps themselves. Like every other German at the time, the Quandts followed the details of the police search for Schleyer closely, seeing in the kidnapped man's background a mirror of their own, to some extent.

The gang took the terrified industrialist to an apartment near Cologne to wait for the heat to die down, before they drove him across the border into Holland. From there, Schleyer was moved on again, this time to neighbouring Brussels, Belgium, and it was from there that the gang continued their demands – they wanted the release of imprisoned members Andreas Baader, Gudrun Ensslin and Jan-Carl Raspe, among others, money and a safe country in which to take refuge.

Then came a new and terrifying twist – four members of the Popular Front for the Liberation of Palestine (PFLP, a faction of the PLO) hijacked Lufthansa flight LH181, which was flying from Palma de Mallorca to Frankfurt on 13 October 1977. Proclaiming solidarity with the RAF, they demanded the release of their German 'comrades', the captured Baader–Meinhoff gang members. The hostage drama continued for five days as the aircraft was denied a number of landing clearances at airports across Arabia before it was finally able to touch down on a sand strip in Aden, Yemen.

Taking full advantage of this new crisis, the RAF added to their demands the release of two Palestinian prisoners. The jet eventually flew on to Somalia and during the tense negotiations the hijackers shot and killed the pilot of the aircraft, Captain Jurgen Schumann. When his body was tossed onto the tarmac Germany's anti-terrorist unit,

GSG-9, stormed the aircraft, killing three of the hijackers but managing to rescue all 86 passengers. Germany's political leaders hoped that this strong response and ultimately successful outcome would serve as a warning to all terrorists.

There was to be further drama, however, which essentially handed the captured Schleyer his death sentence: Baader, Ensslin and Raspe were found dead in their cells in Stammheim Prison, while a fourth member of RAF, Irmgard Moller was discovered seriously injured. It was claimed that they had somehow got hold of a pistol and had committed suicide by shooting themselves, but even today that conclusion is questioned.

The deaths spurred Schleyer's kidnappers into action. On 18 October 1977, Schleyer was driven into France, where he was shot dead near Mulhouse. His body was found later in the trunk of an Audi 100. After that event, the gang seemed to decide to lay low. Just for how long, no-one was sure, leading Germany's rich and powerful to remain both nervous and cautious.

The Quandts were among this group and security around Susanne, her brother and other family members was consequently increased even further. No-one left the luxury Quandt villa in Bad Homburg without an armed escort.

The Quandt family had been warned by police that with more millionaires – in their case billionaires – per capita in the country, Bad Homburg was a kidnapper's dream. Bad Homburg vor der Höhe, meaning 'before the heights' because it is situated at the foot of the Taunus mountains, has been popular with kings, queens, princes and all manner of celebrities over the years. Today the very rich and directors and employees of Frankfurt's banks reside there, happy to live in a town that became famous as far back as 1888, when Kaiser Wilhelm II declared Bad Homburg's schloss – castle – an imperial summer residence. He funded the building of the Church of the Redeemer. Queen Victoria's eldest daughter lived there for a number of years and King Edward VII stayed there from time to time and it was the king who is said to have introduced the Homburg hat and permanent turn-up trousers to the area.

The Quandt family was advised to be careful by GSG–9 itself, advice that several private security companies had also issued. But life had to go on. Susanne and her brother had to go to high school. Their father, the legendary industrialist Herbert Quandt, who had turned a failing BMW company into the luxury vehicle giant of today, had to go about his business. His wife, Johanna, who was destined, along with Susanne and Stefan, to inherit his holdings on his death, had to continue her daily affairs.

But even the best intelligence can fail. A last minute piece of luck saved Susanne and Johanna Quandt from falling into the hands of a desperate gang of criminals. Susanne was 16 at the time and the year was 1978 – just 12 months on from the murder of Hanns-Martin Schleyer and the controversial 'suicides' of the Baader–Meinhof leaders. Police knew that other gang members were still at large and could strike anywhere, at any time, so added security was given to every wealthy family, particularly in and around Frankfurt where the Baader–Meinhof gang had taken root.

Perhaps surprisingly though, it was not the Baader–Meinhof gang who were the threat to the Quandts. A group of 14 prisoners on day release from a local jail had got hold of weapons and believing that they had the firepower and the element of surprise to pull it off, they planned to kidnap the teenage Susanne and her 52-year-old mother. The ransom demand was to be US $20 million. No other details have been released by the authorities, but it is known that the plan was only foiled at the last minute after the police came to hear of it.

Susanne and her mother were safe it seemed – but for how long? There were too many unknowns and Susanne had to continue her studies under the strictest security. Her watchdogs even persuaded Susanne to change her name to the similar-sounding 'Kant' while she continued her education and gained a degree in business finance.

Right up to the end of her studies, Susanne was regarded by her former classmates as charming and friendly, but shy – a result of them misreading a coy demeanour that was largely, in fact, fuelled by caution. Susanne had been warned that revealing details of her personal life even to her teenage friends could lead to problems: they might, in all fairness, harmlessly tell their parents about her, perhaps, and those same 'innocent' particulars might end up as vital information for potential kidnappers.

It was not always locked doors for Susanne, however. She enjoyed skiing holidays with her parents and her brother in the Alps and there were summer vacations in the South of France. The omnipresent security men went with them, of course – and the knowledge that no-one could be truly trusted. Be polite to strangers but never open up to them – that was the Quandt rule.

With her degree behind her, Susanne joined the Young & Rubicam advertising agency in Frankfurt, when she was 19. This was seen as a compromise with her family as her father had wanted her to go into investment banking and she had hoped to make a career in architecture. Susanne remained with the firm for two years but, in 1982, a family tragedy occurred that made further business, banking and management studies essential. Her almost-blind father, Herbert Quandt, the man who built up BMW to stand among the ranks of the world's best vehicle manufacturers, died in June of that year, just three weeks before his 72nd birthday.

As Susanne stood with her mother and brother at his graveside in the forest cemetery near Bad Homburg, she was aware that she had inherited a 50.1 percent stake in the pharmaceutical and chemicals company Altana. Even more importantly, Herbert Quandt left his daughter with a 12.5 percent stake in BMW, although the largest shareholding went to Susanne's mother.

Despite her new-found wealth, Susanne was not content to rest on her laurels. Much more work had to be done and she headed for the UK, where she studied a course in marketing and management at the University of Buckingham, Britain's only private university. The business faculty was located in a number of buildings dating back to the 17th century in the centre of the town of Buckingham near the River Great Ouse. Susanne is said to have felt very much at ease among the mix of British and international students, the majority of whom were from wealthy homes.

Well aware that her future lay with BMW, Susanne sought to improve her business skills and followed her time at Buckingham with a Master of Business Administration (MBA) at the renowned International Institute for Management Development on the shores of Lake Geneva in Lausanne, Switzerland. After that, it was back to London, to work in the branch of Germany's Dresdner Bank. She would have been well aware that Jürgen Ponto, the bank's chief executive had been shot dead close to her Bad Homburg home some 10 years before – yet another reminder that she herself remained under threat, despite the pseudonym she was using. Her skills at the bank opened a new door with the global management consultants McKinsey in Munich, before she moved on yet again, this time to the private bank Reuschel & Co., part of the Dresdner Bank, which looked after very wealthy clients.

Susanne's studies and the various jobs she undertook in finance, advertising and business management removed any remaining doubts that she was an 'idle little rich kid', who had spent her earlier years waiting around to inherit the family fortune.

Susanne and her brother were groomed from a young age to take on what would be among the highest profile jobs in Europe – after all, the time would come when their mother would step aside. To that end, Susanne was given some on-the-job training at the BMW factory in Regensburg, 106km (66 miles) from Munich, where the headquarters are located. Again, she worked under an assumed name.

An elegant, attractive woman with short-cropped blonde hair and – ironically, perhaps – the same blue-grey eyes as the man who was later to betray her, Susanne was aware she had to be very careful about any would-be suitor. Anyone knowing her identity might well just be after her money rather than her hand. So when she went about her traineeship at the BMW factory her fellow workers knew her only as Susanne Kant. Among them was Jan Klatten, an engineer, seven years older than the young girl, a man who had no idea that the alluring woman working 'under cover' in the works canteen at one time, with whom he began flirting, actually owned 12.5 percent of the company.

A DANGEROUS ERA

Warned time and again by her family and security experts to be careful, Susanne wasn't going to let on who she was as she chatted with Jan over cups of coffee and later shared meals with him in Danube-side restaurants and enjoyed drinks in the beer gardens of Regensburg city's old town.

'*I wanted to find out if he really loved me,*' she confided to a friend.

When it became apparent that he did, Susanne took the bold decision, after seven months of seeing one another, to reveal her true identity. Jan was stunned, but he assured her that her wealth and power would make no difference to him – he would love and care for her no matter who she was.

They were married in the spring of 1990 in the Austrian Tyrol – in the ornate, Baroque-style parish church in the mediaeval city of Kitzbühel. The old town sits beside the river Kitzbühler Ache and is a popular ski resort but at this time of the year the mountain slopes were lush with greenery. The newly-weds enjoyed a short honeymoon but Susanne wanted to continue her business studies, this time in Boston, so she and her husband moved there for a year, during which time Jan also took a postgraduate business course. He was determined not to be just the husband of a multi-billionairess.

In 1993, Susanne joined the board of Altana and helped transform the company into an internationally renowned corporation that 11 years later would be able to boast a revenue of US $4 billion. But it was a tougher ride at BMW: in 1994 the German giant bought the British car company Rover for £800 million – a move the business world considered to be a mistake, for Rover was described at the time as being 'very sick'.

It was in 1997 that the matriarch, Johanna, stepped aside to allow Susanne and her brother to be appointed to the supervisory board of the company, although she still retained 16.7 percent of BMW. They agreed that they had to be rid of Rover, particularly after the company received a barrage of criticism from private shareholders at its year–2000 annual general meeting.

One shareholder described the 1994 deal to purchase the British company as the worst investment decision in Germany's history: the money was pouring out of BMW in a torrent. The decision made by Susanne and her brother saw the removal of Bernd Pischetsrieder as CEO and Rover was sold to a British consortium for the symbolic sum of US $10.

By now Susanne was the mother of three children, living with Jan in the arty Schwabing district of Munich. Nestled among its theatres and museums were shops that catered for the wealthy, but it also had the largest park in Europe, the Englischer Garten, with long walking and cycling tracks. She could stroll there in anonymity with her children, a nanny and a discreet bodyguard, for she was determined to maintain the anonymity that she had managed to enjoy throughout her life. Those who did recognize her simply saw a woman in casual clothing – jeans and flats perhaps – certainly no-one making any effort to flash her wealth around.

While members of the BMW board travelled about in chauffeur-driven limousines, Susanne tried as much as possible to drive herself around in a sky-blue Mini. And, while the company executives had the use of a Gulfstream V jet, Susanne preferred to do the opposite, flying around Europe on budget airlines.

If she attended a social event, Susanne and her minders tried to avoid photographs being taken and, if possible, there would be no mention of her in the gossip columns. She avoided mixing with too many people at formal dinners, unless she knew them well and trusted them. If the name Klatten did appear in the diary pages of newspapers and magazines, it was almost always a reference to Werner Klatten, the older half-brother of Jan and head of a TV company.

Susanne was a woman in total control. She had helped save BMW, just as her father had saved the Bavarian company from collapse in 1957, and turned it into a world automobile power. Under the supervision of Susanne and her brother, the company soared so that by 2003, BMW made more money than DaimlerChrysler, Volkswagen and Ford put together. The company's 104,000 employees felt safe with Susanne at the helm.

'*We create peace there, which is essential,*' she told a close friend.

The most powerful businesswoman in Germany, Susanne Klatten

had proved just what an astute player she was – which left the whole of Europe wondering in years to come how on earth that shy and cautious woman had placed at risk everything that she had – her good name, her family, even her company's reputation – for a desperate fling with a smooth-talking man, who was little more than a prostitute.

But it was not that disastrous episode that was to first thrust the very private Susanne Klatten into the limelight. It was her family's alleged Nazi past. For decades the family had tried to ignore it. But towards the end of 2007, the Nazi associations of the Quandt family had come back to haunt them. And, it could not have returned at a worse time for Susanne – for by then she was deeply entangled in the web that had been spun by Helg Sgarbi.

A DARK HISTORY

In his preparations for what he believed was the greatest of all his stings, Helg Sgarbi was aware of two contrasting facts about the woman he was determined to seduce – that while Susanne Klatten was blessed by birth to become an heiress, she was also cursed by her family's dark past.

Her grandfather, Günther Quandt, had served as an adviser to Adolf Hitler, keeping the Führer informed about his factories' operations and their role in the German war machine. This was perfect in itself, Helg realized, but there was also so much more. There were further connections between the Quandt family and the machiavellian Dr Joseph Goebbels and there were also too many witnesses still living for the BMW family to deny the deaths that had occurred in Günther Quandt's munitions factories during the war years.

Günther's factories had made batteries for Germany's U-boats and when his second wife, Magda, divorced him she married Goebbels, Hitler's brilliant propaganda minister. Hitler himself was present at the wedding, as was Günther. Harald (Susanne's great-uncle), the son that Günther had had with Magda, was subsequently brought up by Goebbels and his new wife. Herbert, Günther's son from an earlier marriage, and the man who was to become Susanne's father, went on to take control of the BMW company which Günther had created.

Susanne's background was a complicated one of affairs and divorces to which she was connected by little more than an accident of birth. But because most Germans were not presented with the true facts they had unfairly linked Susanne's own business dealings directly back to Hitler himself.

It had been well established that during the war years, BMW, like other prominent German firms, used slave labour from the concentration camps but the Quandts' other historical links to the Nazi era were hazy because the family had never publicly spoken of them.

Helg, researching the Quandt family, guessed that Susanne had been warned that the subject of her grandfather's alleged Nazi association would arise periodically and that she, like her mother, had resolved to ignore any scandal. As the years passed by, the stigma would surely all fade away. But, as it happened, fate was to work out in Helg's favour.

As if it were not enough that Susanne – so dignified and transparent in the eyes of the German nation – was to start deceiving her husband and was soon to become the victim of Helg's elaborate blackmail plot, her own family's connections to Hitler's brutal rule were finally exposed in the revelatory TV documentary *Das Schweigen der Quandts* ('*The Silence of the Quandts*'). Aired on the German public broadcast channel NDR at 11.30pm on Sunday 30 September 2007, the programme revealed how Susanne's grandfather, Günther Quandt, had built up a fortune using slave labour during World War II and had somehow managed to avoid any post-war recrimination.

None of the Quandt family saw the actual broadcast, but when they learned about it on the following day they were deeply disturbed. It did not help that the newspapers ran headlines such as '*A Fortune Stained in Blood*' and '*The Quandts' Bloody Billions*'.

A copy of the hour-long programme was provided to the reclusive family and Susanne, her brother and their mother watched with increasing alarm as the accusations about slave labour poured from the mouths of survivors. Old men spoke of unbearable conditions and atrocities taking place at Günther Quandt's company, which, along with munitions, had made highly specialized batteries for German submarines and V–2 rockets.

'*We were treated terribly and had to drink water from the toilets,*' said one survivor, Takis Mylopoulos, who worked in the Hanover plant. '*We were also whipped.*'

Then there was the account given by 82-year-old Carl-Adolf Soerensen, a former Danish resistance fighter, who was deported in 1943 and ended up in a concentration camp near the city of Hanover.

He was forced to work at the nearby AFA (Accumulatoren–Fabrik AG) plant owned by Günther Quandt. Soerensen told how he and 40 other forced labourers assembled batteries for submarines. They had to handle toxic-heavy metals, even though they were not provided with any protective clothing. In the first weeks, he said, six people died from lead poisoning and he was informed by SS officers that inmates couldn't expect to survive for more than six months in such conditions.

The filmmakers, Barbara Siebert and Eric Friedler, unearthed documents during their five-year research to make the film, showing that Günther Quandt estimated '*a fluctuation of 80 prisoners a month*' in the battery factory. This was believed to indicate the amount of deaths that could be expected in that time. It was claimed in the documentary, however, that at the AFA factories in Hanover, Berlin and Vienna, prisoners from concentration camps died by the hundreds. In 1972, Soerensen claimed that he had returned to Germany to beg for financial support from the Quandts because he was by then suffering from sickness resulting from his work at the battery plant. He was turned away.

Benjamin Ferencz, a prosecutor from the Nuremberg Trials, which were held after the war to try war criminals, was interviewed in the documentary. He stated that on the basis of the facts uncovered, Günther Quandt should have been convicted of war crimes.'*Quandt escaped justice,*' said Ferencz, who contrasted Günther's lack of punishment with the seven years handed out to the industrialist Friedrich Flick at Nuremberg for similarly using slave labour and for serving the Nazi war machine.

Watching it, said a family friend, was '*a nightmare*' for the Quandts. They had always remained silent about their past, turning down any requests by historians or other commentators seeking to peruse the family's archives.

Whatever Susanne's thoughts as she watched her family's murky history recalled in such a public manner, the timing of the broadcast could not have come at a worse time for her. *This* was a public scandal – but her own secret, should it ever emerge, would make even bigger headlines – of that she was certain. Her immediate reaction, though, was to deal with the problem at hand. There were three options – take legal action, deny it all or fight it through the courts. That said, there was another … to accept that it had all happened and try to make amends for the past. In other words, go into damage-control mode.

Asking their lawyers to issue denials would be futile, the Quandts agreed. Historians had already connected the Holocaust, the Third Reich and AFA to one another, and, even journalist Rüdiger Jungbluth, who had published a book about the family, had made reference to that link.

Besides which, there was one more powerful reason for damage-control. A Quandt family member had already come close to making a full admission about their culpability when he appeared in the documentary. '*We must finally try to forget this,*' said Sven Quandt, Susanne's cousin. He went on to say that he had inherited a fortune from a company that emerged from the battery company AFA, but he wasn't interested in being reminded of what had happened then. He added: '*Every family has its dark sides.*' His words left his relatives, who had previously refused to comment on that part of their past, reeling.

Susanne's brother, Stefan had, in fact gone to some lengths to reinvent his grandfather's public image by describing him as an innovative businessman. In a very rare public appearance at the Karlsruhe's Technical University, in 2001, he told how Günther had '*expanded our family's entrepreneurial thinking and action by investing in companies. His strategy was diversification*'.

As for his own father, Herbert Quandt, who among his many roles had been the director of personnel for the AFA company, Stefan kept it short, stating only that: '*Perhaps my father's most outstanding entrepreneurial feat was to save BMW*' – a reference to Herbert's acquisition of a large package of shares in BMW in 1960, which thereby protected the company from a Daimler–Benz takeover.

A week passed before the Quandt family issued a public response to the documentary – a week in which the phones had run hot between Bad Homberg, Munich and other places where relatives and advisers resided. The Quandts were among the last of Germany's major business owners to confront the dark secrets of their past; they had simply hoped it would all go away if they remained quiet enough. But with class-action law suits looming in the United States, corporate giants like Daimler–Benz, VW, Allianze and Deutsche bank had paid large sums into the German Economy Foundation Initiative formed in 2001 to compensate former slave labourers. Compensation had already been discussed, in fact, two years earlier, following the 1999 founding by BMW, in collaboration with other German companies, of the Remembrance, Responsibility and Future Foundation. But on a personal level the Quandts had, until the documentary was aired, maintained their silence.

The Quandts' response was now to announce that they would back a research project into the family's Nazi past and the role it had played in the Third Reich. The family archives and all documents would also be made available to an independent historian.

'*The accusations that have been raised against our family have moved us,*' said the family in a statement. '*We recognize that our history as a German business family, [in] the years 1933 to 1945, [has] not been sufficiently cleared up.*'

BMW (known during the war years as Bayerische Motoren Werke AG) was implicated with Günther in building its fortune on the blood, sweat and tears of slave labourers. But the focus remained on the Quandts, who became major shareholders in the company 15 years after the war. Arguably, without Günther Quandt's vision, the fortunes of the company could have been quite different.

In order to understand how Susanne Quandt came to be so associated with Hitler, Goebbels and the Nazi regime – and why Helg Sgarbi also told other people that Susanne's family had caused great suffering to his Jewish grandfather – it is necessary to look back to her grandfather's time and follow the events that would lead to such confusion, myth and misconceptions in Susanne's lifetime, more than 50 years later ...

* * *

In 1918, when she was 17, a blonde schoolgirl, riding on a train, became engaged in conversation with a fellow passenger, old enough to be her father. The stranger was called Günther Quandt, a wealthy industrialist who had made money out of supplying uniforms to the German Army during World War I. A widower, Günther had recently lost his wife, Antonie, to the Spanish flu. After meeting the girl, Magda Friedlaender, on that train, Günther began calling on her at school, courting her while posing as a family friend so that the staff there would not become alarmed.

Günther had two sons from his first marriage: Helmut, aged 13, and Herbert (Susanne's father), aged 11, at the time, but Magda was happy to take on the responsibility of the boys when she finally accepted Günther's proposal. The wedding took place in January 1921: Magda was aged 20 and Günther, 40. Their first child, Harald, was born in November of that year and Günther was now the proud father of three boys.

Magda's marriage to Günther was unhappy from the start. Her husband was always away and the young Magda was desperate for company. Günther's sons, Helmut and Herbert, the boys she had become stepmother to so eagerly, were now away being schooled and Magda was lonely and began to look around for company. There are even some suggestions that Magda was attracted to her stepson, Helmut, and it is possible they began an affair, when the young man was 18, but that is conjecture.

In 1927, Günther – and Magda – suffered great loss when Helmut, to whom Magda is alleged to have been so attracted, developed appendicitis and died: he was just 19 years old. Shocked and heartbroken, Magda went on a six-month motoring tour of America, travelling in their red Mayback car. By that point, it was obvious Magda's marriage to Günther wasn't working out and they had discussed a divorce. It was not long before Magda caught the eye of a nephew of former US president Herbert Hoover. However, while they were driving together they were involved in a car crash in which Magda was seriously injured. Although she recovered, discussions that Madga and Hoover's nephew had had about a future together fell by the wayside. Her thoughts of starting a new life in America with him were over.

With their marriage over, Magda and Günther divorced in 1929. It was amicable enough, though, for Günther to ensure that Magda received a large sum of money to see her through the coming years. The couple agreed to share custody of their son, Harald, and Magda also agreed to provide a home for a time for 19-year-old Herbert, Günther's son from his first marriage, although he was already involved with his father's business affairs.

Single once more and desperately lonely, Magda joined the National Socialist Party (the Nazi Party), which was gaining such popularity in Germany at the time. At one of its meetings, she met and later fell in love with one of the main speakers and leading party members, Dr Joseph Goebbels. There are suggestions that Magda also met Adolf Hitler at that time and was actually attracted to him, but since Hitler intended to stay single, her marriage to Goebbels was arranged for the sake of the party. It was even suggested that as the wife of a leading Nazi official she could ultimately serve as the equivalent of the 'first lady' of the Third Reich.

Magda and a hollow-faced Goebbels, his dark hair swept straight back from his forehead, were married in 1931 at Günther's farm in Mecklenburg. Adolf Hitler was among the witnesses present.

It is believed that this was the first time that Günther and Hitler's paths crossed. They chatted amicably. Hitler was working hard to develop working relations with major German industrialists, but Günther seemingly was not all that impressed, describing Hitler as 'thoroughly average'.

Magda subsequently sought and won sole custody of Harald, who gained Goebbels as his stepfather. It is this connection to Goebbels – not a blood link, but that Susanne's grandfather's ex-wife married Goebbels – which was one of the major factors tainting the reputation of the modern Quandts, Susanne included. In the meantime, Günther's other son, Herbert, went to work in one of his father's companies.

From the time that he was appointed as Minister of Propaganda in 1933, Goebbels took total control of Germany's media but he also organized many atrocious attacks on German Jews. Worst among them, perhaps, was what was to become known as the *Kristallnacht* (literally 'Crystal Glass') – a reference to the broken glass that littered the streets after the Pogram of 9 October 1938, when scores of synagogues were razed to the ground and hundreds of Jews were assaulted or murdered.

It was Goebbels' excellently run propaganda machine that prepared the German people, psychologically at least, for war and the subsequent brutal slaughter of civilian populations which were a part of Hitler's great plan for world domination.

Over time, Günther Quandt came to change his opinion of Hitler; he joined the Nazi party following the Führer's election as Chancellor in January 1933. In turn, he was rewarded with the position of Leader of the Armament Economy, an honour afforded to industrialists playing an important part in the war economy. Historian Ralf Blank was to describe him as '*one of the most important German arms' producers*' of the time.

Susanne's grandfather was one of many German industrialists who appropriated factories throughout Europe in the wake of the Nazi army's successful sweep across the continent. And, like many others, Günther's factories were filled with forced labour brought in from the concentration camps.

While Goebbels and Günther were not the greatest of friends, when the latter was arrested in 1933, Goebbels put in a good word for him with Hitler and Günther was subsequently released.

Hitler himself is said to have been fascinated with Magda. As early as 1931, he is alleged to have said: '*This woman could play an important role in my life, even without being married to her. In all my work, she could represent the female counterpart to my one-sided male instincts.*' Such was the trust that Hitler placed in Magda that after a failed attempt to poison him at the Kaiserhof Hotel in Berlin in January 1933, Adolf asked Magda to prepare all his meals for him.

As for her marriage, although Magda had six children with Goebbels, all of whom Hitler served as godfather to, Magda became disillusioned with her second husband. She was also aware that Goebbels was having affairs, including a long and not-so-secret relationship with the popular Czech actress Lida Baarova, who was not unlike Magda in looks.

It was inevitable that such a high-profile affair would reach Magda's attention. And, when it did, the first person that Magda turned to for advice was Hitler. The Führer is alleged to have ordered Goebbels to end the affair, but Goebbels was so smitten with the actress that he offered his resignation, telling Hitler that he wanted a divorce and would marry Lida and emigrate to Japan. Hitler refused to accept his resignation, although he was so angry about Goebbels' betrayal of Magda that he did consider sending Goebbels to Japan in any case as German ambassador. Ultimately, Goebbels was 'grounded' and had to remain in Germany.

Lida was informed that she was a *persona non grata* in Germany and was ordered to leave. After the war she faced a death sentence for collaborating with the Germans, but she was able to prove that she had left the country before the war even started. She was given a prison sentence, nonetheless, but she continued to work in films after her release, appearing in Fellini's 1953 classic *I vitelloni*. Stricken with Parkinson's disease, she died alone in Salzburg in 2000. She still had a few kind words to express about Goebbels before her death, describing him as 'an interesting character' who was both charming and intelligent.

Magda, in the meantime, had decided that what was good enough for her husband was good for her too. She began her own affairs, including one with Karl Hanke, Goebbels' deputy and the Propaganda Ministry's State Secretary. Hitler had had enough, however – just as he'd stepped in to end Goebbels' affair with Lida, he ordered Hanke to essentially 'back off'.

Despite their own disagreements, Magda and Goebbels remained loyal to Hitler as the war descended. But Magda began to worry increasingly that the dictator was too strong-headed to see that his plans for world domination were on shaky ground. In November 1942, when the war started to turn against the German army on the eastern front, she sat with a group of friends listening to the Führer make a speech.

'*My God, what a load of rubbish,*' she is alleged to have exclaimed. '*He doesn't listen to the voices of reason any more. He only listens to people who tell him what he wants to hear.*'

Harald Quandt, who had split his childhood days between his father Günther and with Magda and Goebbels, remained with Magda until he passed his school leavers' exams in 1940. He was a strong supporter of the Indian nationalist, Subhas Chandra Bose, whose motto was: '*Give me blood and I will give you freedom.*'

Harald fought at the Front as a Luftwaffe pilot during the war and was captured by the Allies in Italy in 1944. Imprisoned for the next three years, he never got to see his brothers and sisters again, due to one of the greatest tragedies of the war – one caused by and carried out by his own mother.

THE SECRET FAMILY

In 1945 Hitler knew it was all over and as a final gesture of kindness he offered his bunker to the Goebbels family as the Red Army began their pillaging of Berlin – looting, raping, slaughtering. The Goebbels were given a room previously occupied by Hitler's personal physician, Theodor Morell, and Hitler allocated the only bathroom in the bunker to Magda and her six children.

'*There is no way out,*' Hitler stated. '*It is over.*'

Magda knew what she had to do, but first she needed to write to Harald, incarcerated as he was in a prisoner of war camp in North Africa. She knew that if he read it, he would understand exactly what she had planned.

> '*My beloved son!*' she wrote. '*By now we have been in the Führerbunker for six days already – daddy, your six little siblings and I, for the sake of giving our national socialistic lives the only possible honourable end …*
>
> '*You shall know that I stayed here against daddy's will and that even on last Sunday the Führer wanted to help me to get out. You know your mother – we have the same blood, for me there was no wavering. Our glorious idea is ruined and with it everything beautiful and marvellous that I have known in my life. The world that comes after the Führer and national socialism is not any longer worth living in and therefore I took the children with me, for they are too good for the life that would follow, and a merciful God will understand me when I will give them the salvation …*
>
> '*The children are wonderful … there never is a word of complaint nor crying. The impacts are shaking the bunker. The elder kids cover the younger ones, their presence is a blessing and they are making the Führer smile once in a while.*

'May God help that I have the strength to perform the last and hardest. We only have one goal left; loyalty to the Führer even in death.

'Harald, my dear son − I want to give you what I learned in life: be loyal! Loyal to yourself, loyal to the people and loyal to your country …

'Be proud of us and try to keep us in dear memory …'

As the Soviet tanks pounded above them, Goebbels dictated his last will and testament to Hitler's secretary, Traudl Junge, in which he stressed that Magda and their children supported him in his refusal to leave Berlin and his determination to die in the bunker. Later, he altered the will to emphasize that the children would support his decision to take his own life should they be old enough to speak for themselves but this would never happen.

On the afternoon of 30 April 1945 − two days after Magda wrote her letter to Harald − Hitler and Eva Braun, the woman whom he had eventually married, committed suicide by swallowing cyanide capsules. On 1 May 1945, Magda's six children were drugged with morphine and died when cyanide capsules were broken in their mouths. There were no witnesses to the actual event, but the most popular opinion holds that SS doctor Ludwig Stumpfegger was responsible for crushing the capsules in the youngsters' mouths. It is equally possible that Magda would have wanted to perform this last, sad act herself, though.

The bodies of the children, dressed in their nightclothes and with ribbons tied neatly in the girls' hair, were found in their bunk beds when Soviet troops stormed into the bunker the following day. The Red Army soldiers found none of the principals alive. *Did any of them struggle?* Bruises on the eldest child, Helga, aged just 12, suggested that she resisted the attempt to poison her, but had been held down. After the death of their children, it is surmised that Magda and Joseph Goebbels made their own way up the stairs to the garden, littered as it was with bricks and roofing from the shelled Reich Chancellery above the bunker, where they ended their own lives.

Accounts of the Goebbels' end have varied through the years since that day, although it seems certain that Magda was shaking uncontrollably, shocked by the murder of her children, whether by her own hand or another's – aware that her own death was just minutes away. One account claims that they each took a cyanide capsule and before the poison took effect that they were shot by an SS soldier. Another suggests that they were machine-gunned to death at their own request, while another raises the possibility that Goebbels shot Magda and then brought the pistol to his own head to end his life.

Whatever the events that led to their actual deaths, someone was certainly on hand to douse the bodies in petrol and burn them. Russian troops found the charred remains on the afternoon of 2 May 1945: enough of Goebbels' face remained for him to be identified. The children were buried by the Soviets but years later were re-interred by the Soviets, cremated, and their ashes were scattered in the River Elbe.

Poor Harald, then, was the only member of Magda's children to survive. Among his keepsakes were his mother's last letter and a family photograph featuring Harald, blond-haired and dressed in his Luftwaffe uniform, standing behind his mother, stepfather Goebbels and stepbrother and five stepsisters, who stare into the camera with him (*see plate 1*).

What then of Herbert in that time? Herbert, who was to start the line that led to Susanne Klatten? Did Herbert know what was going on in his father Günther's factories during the war? The use of forced labour of prisoners from the concentration camps?

There is little doubt that he did, for he had become the director of Pertrix GmbH, a Berlin-based subsidiary of AFA, which is alleged to have used female slave labourers, among them Polish women from the notorious Auschwitz concentration camp.

Herbert was groomed by his father for business and he became a member of the executive board of another of Günther's battery manufacturing factories, Accumulatorenfabrik, later known as Varta, AG, in 1940, before his role in Pertrix GmbH. He proved to be an astute industrialist and he helped his father establish and build the Quandt empire after the end of the war.

After the war, Günther's links with the Nazi regime did result in him being interned, but his detention was relatively short – two years. He had been judged to be a *mitlaüfer* (a 'collaborator').

THE SECRET FAMILY

After he was freed, Günther was able to regain control of the family assets. He was also appointed to the supervisory boards of a number of German firms, including the prestigious Deutsche Bank and he became an honorary citizen of Frankfurt University in 1951, three years before his death while on holiday in Cairo, Egypt.

By the time Günther died, aged 73, the Quandt group of companies numbered some 200, and manufactured batteries, textiles and chemicals – the chemical companies including Altana AG. The group also owned some 10 percent of Daimler–Benz and 30 percent of BMW.

After Günther's demise, the huge conglomerate was split between Herbert and his step-brother, Harald. Herbert concentrated on the battery and automotive investments, while Harald took charge of the tool-making and engineering companies.

Herbert was married several times, the first in 1933 to Ursel Münstermann; they were divorced seven years later. Their daughter remained with her mother while Herbert concentrated on business interests. It was not until 1950 that he married again, this time to a jeweller Lieselotte Blobelt. They raised three children together – Sonja, who was born in 1951, Sabina, who was born two years later, and Sven, born in 1956. But again, Herbert's marriage failed and the couple were divorced in 1959.

It is not surprising perhaps that the marriages came under great strain. Herbert had devoted all his time to his companies and he was particularly worried about BMW, which was leaking money. Quite simply, while its vehicles ran efficiently, their style was tired and out of date. They belonged to an earlier era, well before the war.

The company had a chequered history, particularly during and after the war. Originally set up in 1917 as an aircraft-engine manufacturer – the blue and white logo on today's vehicles represents a propeller – in the 1920s it started making motorcycles, then moved to car manufacture. Günther bought into the company at about that time and when the war began, BMW was pulled into the German war machine and began building engines for the Luftwaffe. The motor-cycle factory in south-east Germany was an obvious target for the invading Red Army in 1945 and what was left after the bombings was confiscated by the Soviets, while the Americans set about dismantling BMW's factories near Munich. The Allies barred the company from producing anything mechanical, except bicycles and kitchenware.

Relief came in the early 1950s when the ban was slowly lifted, but a difficult road lay ahead. BMW had to rebuild its reputation as a car manufacturer but in the postwar years, few Germans could afford even a motor bike, let alone a car. By 1959, the company was on the verge of bankruptcy and Daimler–Benz was poised for a takeover. If that had happened, BMW would have been reduced to being a supplier of car bodies for Mercedes–Benz vehicles.

The crunch came in December of that year, when Hans Feith, who headed BMW's management board, warned his colleagues that the alternatives were bankruptcy or being bought out by 'the enemy', Daimler–Benz. Feith appeared to have a good reason for wanting Daimler–Benz to win the day, for he was also a representative of Deutsche Bank, one of BMW's main creditors.

The BMW board was on the point of giving a show of hands for the Daimler–Benz takeover when a group of disgruntled shareholders managed to win an adjournment. Herbert Quandt, who was among them, had earlier been in favour of the Daimler–Benz acquisition, but he was now listening to the angry trade unions and factory workers, who were threatening strike action. Herbert consulted every banker he knew. They all advised him to sell. But against all warnings that disaster would befall BMW if they held off selling any longer, Herbert began to quietly increase his stake in the company. When he owned almost 50 percent of BMW, he managed to make an agreement with the state of Bavaria, which allowed him to buy out BMW.

With a new-found independence, BMW engineers set to work on models that were already on the drawing board – and it was those designs that became the basis of today's classic cars. Less than two years after the near-collapse of the company, the small, feisty 1500 was launched at the 1961 Frankfurt Motor Show and the fair-haired, near-blind Herbert Quandt was hailed as a hero.

Incredibly, during this time, Herbert found time for romance, although he did not have to look far for a new wife. In 1960, just one year after his divorce from Lieselotte Blobelt, he married his secretary Johanna Bruhn. Johanna was a company woman; she was also Herbert's personal assistant and was destined to inherit a large stake in BMW on his death.

Herbert's stepbrother Harald, meanwhile, after being released from a POW camp, sowed a few seeds and partied with prostitutes, before he settled down to helping Herbert rebuild the family fortune. In 1950, he married Inge Bandekow; Inge's father had been Günther Quandt's lawyer and her mother had been Günther's secretary. Harald found it difficult to settle down, however. A former swashbuckling airman who had endured the rigours of a prisoner of war camp, he began to struggle with life, especially with a modest bride in her early 20s, who was far from worldly wise. On top of that, he had to deal with the collapse of the Third Reich and the murder–suicide of his mother, Magda, and his young half siblings – while also concentrating on helping his step-brother Herbert in business.

He fell into deep depression and his deep moods had a negative effect on Inge, who also turned to anti-depressants. Just as his stepbrother Herbert had found it difficult to mix business with domestic duties, the same applied to Harald. He found a mistress in West Berlin but also made time to visit prostitutes.

Somehow, Harald's marriage struggled on: he and Inge had five daughters over the next 17 years. Their fifth daughter, Patricia, was born in 1967, then tragedy struck – a few week's after her birth, Harald was killed in a plane crash in Saluzzo, Italy. Inge moved from partner to partner before marrying a banker. She died of a heart attack on Christmas Eve 1978, and two days later her husband shot himself in their bedroom.

Against this astonishing history of deceit, scandal and great tragedy, Herbert and Johanna settled down into life in leafy Bad Homburg. In order to avoid financial disputes among his various children, Herbert distributed the shares from the various Quandt family companies among them. Silvia, from his first marriage to Ursel, received investments and property while the three children from his second marriage were gifted with the majority of shares in the Varta battery company.

BMW was, in the meantime, now going from strength to strength. Herbert had made what was seen as a brilliant decision in appointing Eberhard von Künheim as managing director and he revamped the car manufacturer into a premium vehicle builder, one that was to seriously challenge Mercedes–Benz.

Herbert continued to increase his stake in BMW, thus ensuring that his first child with Johanna was assured of a future free of financial worry. On 28 April 1962, Susanne Hanna Ursula Quandt came into the world and her brother Stefan joined her four years later, on 9 May 1966. As they grew up their father was increasingly beset by ill-health. By the time he died, Herbert's business was worth a fortune and Johanna, Susanne and Stefan inherited dozens of firms with annual turnovers of 6.5 billion euros and a 49 percent of BMW's shares.

Johanna became the most powerful person in the company. She took control of the family's shares and took her late husband's seat on the advisory board. Despite her ascendency to this position, she continued to keep her family away from the public eye. Whether Johanna was worried that the press would discover the family links to the Nazis is not known, but it is more likely that she was aware that their great wealth – now billions – could make them a potential target for criminals and she was protecting her children. The less the outside world knew about them, the better – should a TV crew turn up outside the gates of their luxury villa, it was quickly given short-shrift by the Quandt security guards. TV crews today have numerous clips of security guards hurrying towards the camera, followed by a hand smothering the lens.

From the very beginning, claimed a family friend, '*Johanna was a very purposeful, confident woman, as you might expect from someone who had spent so many years with Herbert, rising up through the ranks from his humble secretary to become one of the richest women in Germany. But she was also very, very careful, almost to the point of being fanatical.*' In fact, she told close friends that there were two things that were important in life – to remain private and not waste money.

After the failed kidnapping plot in 1978, Johanna is alleged to have disguised herself whenever she ventured outside and even, in more recent years, she is believed to have dressed up as a maid to go outdoors and she rarely spoke to strangers.

In 1997 she stood down from the advisory board and handed control of her shares to Susanne, aged 35, and to Stefan. Despite this, Johanna still maintained a hands-on approach to the company's affairs. In 2000, aged 72, she was still going to her office every day, working late into the evening before returning to the privacy of her villa. She drove a BMW, of course, but should she need to fly somewhere, she still bought an economy ticket – something Susanne inherited from her.

★ ★ ★

Thus, there was a legacy of silence among the Quandts. They never gave interviews and avoided being photographed, even at social events. Should they entertain at home, their guests were carefully handpicked.

A guest at one of the Quandt parties once described them as being socially reserved to an unusual degree. '… *what struck me as unusual is that, even when they are the hosts, the Quandts seldom circulate among guests. They just sit at their table, talking quietly among themselves while others enjoy their hospitality.*'

Even after her own marriage to Jan, Susanne lived a purposefully sheltered life, although she attended charity balls, skied and played at the iconic Bad Homburg Golf Club – but these activities escaped the eyes of the society press. The births of Susanne's three children also managed to evade the gossip columns. She was an invisible woman to everyone but a very close circle of loyal friends. One of this group described Susanne as a '*very down-to-earth woman when she is with those she trusts. If she doesn't know you, she'll be polite, but dismissive.*'

Mysterious, even cautious, Susanne Klatten, née Quandt, had built a secure wall around herself, guarding her family and its mysteries. Some of those close to Susanne describe her as looking like the brilliant German actress Corinna Harfouch, who, ironically played Günther Quandt's second wife, Magda, in the German film classic *Downfall*, which detailed the last days of Hitler and the people with whom he shared his bunker.

PART TWO
The Gigolo and the Guru

PLAYING THE FIELD

They were literally dragged off the streets – 12 million people from nearly 20 countries the Germans had conquered across Europe, and herded into factories to work for the Nazi war machine. Others were marched at gunpoint out of prison camps to bolster the ranks of slave labour. At the top of the list were those deemed '*the undesirables*' – Jews, communists, criminals, homosexuals and the homeless.

In those dark and crowded factories, many prayed they would be sent back to the prison camps where life was kinder, for food in those sweat shops was short and people dropped dead from illness and fatigue. German companies, at least 2,000 of them, could not get enough of the 'free' workforce – many of whom were seen by the Nazis as 'sub-human' – and if deaths reduced the number of these degenerates, the bosses could simply ask for more.

Most of the concentration camps were nothing more than 'waiting rooms' for the gas chambers, or a source of labour for the factories that fed the Nazi war machine. It could go either way – for some of the pitiful inmates were drawn from camps all around Germany, one of which was the Mittelbau–Dora labour camp that provided workers to help with the production of the V–2 rocket. Many of these inmates ended up in the factory that made batteries for these rockets – the AFA factory owned by Günther Quandt.

This was a perfect background for the man who was to plan one of the greatest cons that Europe has seen in recent years. This grim period in German history would provide a perfect cover for the scam. That was, of course, if it all went wrong – and he really couldn't imagine that it would.

Russak. That was the name that he was born with and there were enough Jews of that name who were forced to work in the factories, sceptics claimed, to bring some credence to his audacious claims later, whether they were true or not.

★   ★   ★

At home, his middle-class parents spoke to him in German as he grew up, but out in the streets it was a different language that filled his ears – Portuguese. Helg Russak's father, Steffen had taken a job as the head of Brazilian arm of the Swiss engineering company Sulzer, which was located in Rio. There was perhaps some irony in this, for Brazil, and other South American countries, had become the refuge of choice for Nazis fleeing Germany after the war. At least eight prominent Nazis made Brazil their new home, among them Josef Mengele, the man responsible for the deaths of thousands at Auschwitz, many in the sickening experiments he conducted on prisoners with genetic abnormalities.

Although Helg attended a German school – which placed an emphasis on both the German language and Portuguese – and also an international school, he grew up resenting Rio. Certainly, he went to the beach, made friends and always displayed the best of manners, but he was to complain years later that his childhood had been stolen from him – that he had been denied the chance to grow up in his native Switzerland, among children from the same background. He was to tell friends that he had a '*lot of catching up*' to do on his return to Europe.

Helg and his younger sister returned with their parents to Switzerland for visits, from time to time, but it was not until Helg was in his early teens that the family packed their bags and returned to Switzerland for good. His father had been appointed assistant director at the Sulzer's Winterthur plant, where his career was to go from strength to strength. He worked at developing a new pump system, for which he filed for a patent in 1983. Meanwhile Helg attended the local secondary school before moving on to the local Kantonssschule – the Canton School, where most of the girls fell for the slim, dark-haired teenager who walked through the corridors with such an air of confidence.

The school boasted of providing a broad, balanced education, with a goal that was '*the simultaneous promotion of intellectual talent, willpower, experience and empathy skills*.' Close to parkland, it was a perfect place for a young romantic – for it was evident to his fellow students that was how Helg saw himself – and he made the most of it.

One of Helg's former girlfriends has described him as the '*kind of guy you usually only find in novels*.' Now embarrassed to have strolled hand-in-hand along the tracks beside the Rheinfalls, the largest waterfall in Europe and just 10 minutes drive from Winterthur, the woman who calls herself 'Marian Schneider' describes him as tall and taut, with powerful shoulders from visits to the ski slopes. He was in a class below her but that did not stop her falling for him. To other pupils, they just looked right together ... the pretty 18-year-old blonde and the 17-year-old youth.

> '*His manners were impeccable*,' she remembers. '*When we were walking in the street, he made sure he was on the outside, just like the old-fashioned way. At every door he was there to hold it open for me and he made sure that if he had to leave me in town for any reason he would pay for my taxi fare home.*
>
> '*I asked him around to dinner at the house one evening and my mother was also very impressed with his manners. He was everything a girl could for wish in a man – charming and sophisticated without being arrogant.*'

A photograph taken when he was 17 shows Helg with his long dark hair over his ears, the sleeves of his dark sweater rolled up as he smiles at the camera – and Marian felt, rather like many of the other students, that Helg possessed an almost spiritual aura.

Other students painted a contrasting picture, some recalling an arrogant young man who believed he was better than his peers. Others found that he mixed with people easily and was comfortable talking about all manner of subjects.

PLAYING THE FIELD

∽

Now a successful businessman in Zurich, a former school friend paints a worrying picture today of the young Russak he remembers.

'You always had the feeling that he was going to be big in some way or another later in life. He was a magnet for women, he was pretty clever and above all he was ambitious and confident. You felt that nothing was going to stop him in whatever direction he was going to take when he left school. He made you feel whenever you were with him that he was better than you in all respects. If there were two of you out and about it was always he who was the person in charge, the leader, the one who took control of any situation. Most of us who felt that way now feel justified in reaching that conclusion. He took his arrogance one step too far.'

∽

During school holidays Helg disappeared from Winterthur. Despite the reported strained relations between them, he had travelled with his parents to their second home in the exclusive ski resort of Davos, tucked away in the Alps 150km (93 miles) to the southeast of Winterthur and some 20km (12 miles) from Klosters, the favourite winter retreat of the young British Royals.

He always returned looking the picture of health, tanned – winter and summer – and fighting fit. Just to rent a chalet in Davos can cost more than £2,000 a week, so his father's job was proving to be highly profitable. But Davos was also to be profitable for Helg in another sense, for if anywhere counted as a training ground for mixing with the rich this was it. Famous as a former upper-class health resort, Davos is where Robert Louis Stevenson completed his classic novel *Treasure Island* (1883) while resting in a sanatorium there and where German Nobel Prize–winning writer Thomas Mann spent months while his wife was in a sanatorium, which inspired him to write the 1924 novel *The Magic Mountain*.

In the early 1980s, the teenage Helg might have crossed paths with the many powerful world figures who gathered at Davos each year for the meetings run by the Geneva-based World Economic Forum. An indication of the attraction that the resort still holds for international leaders and celebrities can be seen in its 'guest list' over the years: Bill Gates, Bill Clinton, Al Gore, Nelson Mandela, Angela Merkel, Henry Kissinger – and a name which was to be uttered by Helg, as part of his blackmail plan, in years to come, the Brazilian writer Paulo Coelho. Although Coelho did not start visiting Davos until 1998, his famous novel *The Alchemist*, was to play a brief but major role in the adult Helg Russak's less than salubrious life.

At that time, however, in Davos, he flirted with the daughters of the wealthy, honing his skills. There can be no doubt that he realized how easy it was to turn the heads of the young women who had arrived there from all over the world. It was during these holidays that his confidence with the opposite sex grew. The bars and the nightclubs were filled with multi-millionaires and idle, rich young women, who were there to ski, dance, drink, perhaps even engage in a little bit of romance and perhaps again, just the sex. Most were enamoured with his conversation, for he was already knowledgeable about art and Swiss architecture, and he was adept at all sports that he turned his hand to, whether it be swimming, skiing, sailboarding on the lakes or tennis.

But Helg Russak also had studies to complete, which he did at UZH (University of Zurich). Founded in 1833, it claims to be among the top educational centres in Europe. Among its Nobel Prize laureates are Albert Einstein, Paul Karrer for his research into vitamins and Walter Rudolf Hess, for his studies into the functions of internal organs.

When Russak was there, student numbers in the field of information technology increased to an above-average rate and he was among those who realized that this was to be the way of the future. But in between his studies he was expected to earn his keep – and he found work selling Macdonalds hamburgers in Zurich and making pizzas in another restaurant. Friends knew when he'd been working as he would dab himself with generous doses of aftershave to hide the smell of cooking. His classic looks also led him to be a part-time model for men's clothing. His university friends describe him in the same way as those who knew him at school in Winterthur – as a friendly, outgoing man, polite and self-assured. And, of course, he was always surrounded by beautiful young women, many of whom found their way into his bed at his Zurich lodgings.

∽

'There is no doubt that Helg lost his virginity long before he came to university,' a former university student remembers. 'Perhaps he lost it somewhere up there in the Alps, where there are women by the thousand. You only had to watch the way he moved around the university to know that he was a lot more experienced in talking to the girls than most of the rest of us.'

∽

When he was 22, with a law degree behind him, Helg spent 17 weeks in the Swiss army. Like every other young man he was required to sign on in his late teens and begin national service at the age of 20 but if work or study intervened, men could potentially postpone it until the age of 23. Recruits underwent training at boot camp for up to 21 weeks and it was in the summer of 1987 that Helg found himself sharing a room with Urs Tinner, who was himself to become a colourful character in the eyes of the law.

Police sources believe that the seeds of crime – still unproven in the case of Tinner – were sewn as the two men sat in their camouflage uniforms and talked in the barracks in Bulach, Zurich, about the computer age, women, money and war. Neither man realized at that time, however, that they were each to make headlines, not just in Switzerland, but around the world.

Tinner, along with his younger brother Marco, was imprisoned on suspicion of supplying the secret network of Abdul Qadeer Khan, creator of Pakistan's atomic bomb, with technical advice and equipment in early 2000. In turn, Khan sold the equipment – used to make gas centrifuges – to such countries as Libya and Iran, which were moving ahead with their nuclear weapons programmes.

Khan's activities were monitored by Western intelligence agencies before his operation was disrupted in 2003 with the seizure of nuclear weapons parts being carried on a ship bound for Libya. The Tinner brothers were held under 'investigative detention' by Swiss authorities until 2008, while their alleged activities were probed and by mid 2009 no charges had been laid.

Shortly after his release from prison in December 2008, Urs Tinner told Swiss TV station SF1 that it was he who had tipped off US intelligence about the ship en route to Libya. The CIA declined to confirm or deny suggestions that Urs Tinner had been recruited by them, as early as 2000, but, if these claims were true, observers noted that a public trial could prove to be awkward for the Swiss government, whose officials were said to have destroyed a number of key documents relating to the case, under pressure from the US.

Despite his obvious fitness and his ascension to the rank of lieutenant, Helg Russak was to be dismissed from the military on medical grounds. Friends of Helg in Switzerland said that he had told them that he had been 'released' because of poor eyesight, but there was no official confirmation of this.

In his dark business suit, Helg settled into life as an investment banker at Credit Suisse instead, where he impressed his superiors with his work and his interaction with clients.

Helg learned how to manage large assets as millions upon millions of dollars/pounds passed through his hands before deciding to specialize in mergers and acquisitions. He became an expert at grooming potential investors, a skill that, far away from the bank, he was to employ in the future. But it is likely that even he did not know how useful this skill was going to prove to be as he went about his daily duties.

Beyond the bank's walls, beautiful women fell under his hypnotic spell, seduced by Helg's looks and his obvious intelligence. There was something boyish about him, which had the effect of making him even more beguiling to certain women.

PLAYING THE FIELD

In 1994, at the age of 29, he married one of the girls who was so smitten by his charm, but she quickly became tired of his wandering eyes and the relationship ended after two years. Now he was free to play the field and he was often among the first to be invited whenever a party was being arranged. Hardly a weekend passed when he was not standing in an apartment or a garden with a drink in his hand and a clutch of attractive women around him, among them former friends from his university days. It was at one of these soirées that he met a stocky Italian. He did not share Helg's good looks or endearing charm, but seemed to have no difficulty, either, in surrounding himself with awe-struck women.

Through the crowd Ernani Barretta's dark eyes settled on Helg Russak. He watched him for a while. Then, he threaded his way across the room towards him, hand outstretched.

THE GURU

Two hours drive from Rome, the A25 winds through the Pescara Valley, climbing up to 1,640ft (0.5km) above sea level and there, nestling inside the Laga National Park and within the Abruzzo region in Central Italy, is the spectacular hanging village of Pescosansonesco. The poet Gabriele d'Anunzio, who was born in Pescara, just to the northeast of the village, before his death in 1938, described Pescosansonesco as *an eagle's nest, incredibly built on a cliff, seemingly inaccessible.*

But it is more than its spectacular location on the cliffs that has brought tourists to the village through the decades – once they had found it, for it was so tiny, with a population of just a few hundred, that it was often excluded from the bigger maps. They came, and still come, as pilgrims to pray to the Blessed Nunzio Sulprizio who was beatified in December 1963.

In the early 1800s, Nunzio suffered terrible abuse in his uncle's blacksmith's shed, where he worked the bellows for hours on end and ran errands, all without pay. He begged for food from his neighbours and suffered terrible beatings. Yet, he never complained nor questioned his uncle's authority and in any spare moment, he could be found on his knees, praying. Witnesses said, that despite having an ulcerated foot, caused by his uncle throwing a sledgehammer at him, peace emanated from him. Later, aged 15 – his bones by now calcified, his leg gangrenous, his entire body emaciated – he was rescued by another kinder uncle and he received his first communion. Finally, in 1836, as he lay on his death bed at the age of 19, he turned his eyes to a painting of the Virgin Mary in his room. *'The Virgin Mary!'* he exclaimed. *'See how beautiful she is.'* And then he died.

While in Pescosansonesco, Nunzio is believed to have washed his terrible wounds in a spring behind the village sanctuary, which today is believed to hold miraculous powers. Modern-day pilgrims leave Pescosansonesco filled with hope after hearing his story. Nunzio also inspired another young man, Ernani Barretta, whose life turned out to be far from '*holy*'.

Ernani was born in the '*new village*' of Pescosansonesco, created after the old town was damaged by earthquakes in 1917 and 1933.

From a young age, Ernani heard Nunzio's story time and again and he experienced firsthand some of the poverty that the young saint had lived in. Ernani was one of the 10 children of a strictly Catholic peasant couple who struggled to find enough food to feed them all. But they taught their children to pray and attend church each Sunday and as Ernani grew up he placed all his faith in a miracle that might release him from the difficult world that his parents knew. For a time, he earned pocket money by taking tourists around the mountain village's famous sites, including the ruins of a mediaeval castle and the blacksmith's workshop where Nunzio had once toiled.

Lacking anything more than a basic education, Ernani started working as a mechanic in the village centre, but his eyes frequently sought out the groups of visitors who came to the village to pray at the shrine that had been erected in Nunzio's honour. He realized that there was another world out there, beyond the mountains that surrounded Pescosansonesco.

In his later teens Ernani had a taste of the greater world when he managed at times to slip away from his daily routine in the workshop and travel with a group of friends, all of them on motor scooters, to the seaside town of Pescara, 40km (25 miles) away. There, he not only smelled the sea washing in over 20km (12 miles) of beaches – he also smelled wealth. Looking at the new hotels that had risen up after wartime bombings, he became increasingly convinced that he had to move away from his village if he was to make anything of his life. And, he had one quality that he had come to realize might help him on his way – he possessed a magnetic aura that seemed to draw people to him.

He had first recognized it when he'd shown the pilgrims around in his younger days and he'd seen its power again in Pescara, when he and his friends mixed with strangers in the beachside cafés. People found him easy to talk to, for there appeared to be nothing complicated about him – most saw an easy-going, friendly Italian, others something more, an almost spiritual, perhaps divine aura, emanating from him. Ernani decided that he was going to use whatever this was to his advantage, but he would need to move away from a mountain village to make it work. And if it did, well, perhaps he would return one day and build himself a castle!

He worked for a while in Rome, then headed north-west to the place where he knew the money was – to Zurich. And Beatrice, the wife who he had met as a teenager, came with him.

Barretta started out doing what he knew best, working as a mechanic in a workshop. The wage would have been decent enough for him to rent a small apartment but he and Beatrice decided to save money and so moved in with Beatrice's mother, who lived in Zurich. The money they could put aside, they decided, would give them a start for a more productive future.

Ernani began attending a number of Catholic churches in the city, greeting people, allowing them to experience firsthand his magnetic charm – and to his great pleasure he found that the people reacted as he wanted them to. Whether he sincerely believed he had become imbued with the spirit of Nunzio was something only he knew, but he quickly learned that there was a vast community in the city, all seeking spiritual comfort.

Some time in 1988 after Sunday Mass, he became engaged in conversation with the wife of a lawyer who complained of constant headaches. Barretta took her hands in his and told her that faith was a great healer and that his belief in God's healing would flow into her and heal her. Whether it was the power of positive thinking – even he was not able to explain later – but the next week, he found the woman grasping his hand again, this time to thank him. Her headaches had gone, she exclaimed! Praise poured from the lips of her husband. He could never thank Ernani enough – he had brought calm to their household.

Word spread.

THE GURU

In the following weeks, groups in church congregations sought Ernani Barretta out, if for no other reason than to talk with him. He was not educated enough to discuss the ins and outs of politics or the law or medicine, but those were not the subjects about which they wanted to hear anyway: they wanted to listen to him espouse the power of prayer.

Now Ernani could make use of his poverty-stricken background – and he talked of the tiny holy village, from which he had come, up in the mountains of Italy. His description of the shrine of Nunzio and the holy water only added to the reputation he was gaining as a man who had something special to offer.

For good measure, he claimed that he knew the pain of human suffering as from a young age he had had to walk 10km (6 miles) each day to go to school in the small town of Bolognano and, while still a young boy, he, too, had toiled for hours on end in the local blacksmith's shop. He had worked in Rome and he had travelled to Argentina and Spain, he told them, where he had learned of good and evil. His personal sacrifices were beyond measure.

In Zurich, he would visit the homes of people with strong religious convictions who believed that they would benefit from this mysterious, yet charismatic man from the mountains of Italy laying his hands on them. He wore loose clothing – creating an impression of freedom – and spoke softly of God's love and how he had been chosen to help others.

As the weeks, then the months, rolled by, Ernani realized that there was money to be made in religion – through the gullibility of others. He was happy to accept donations from the wealthy, those people who believed that they had benefited, either in body or mind, from meeting with him. Those people who did not give a thought to the power of suggestion. Gradually his bank balance began to swell.

A house was found where a small group of strong believers gathered. Ernani spoke of the importance of loving each other and of the need to be spiritual. Although he attracted professional people, academics from the university began turning up with students and Ernani saw how the women, in particular, seemed attracted to him.

They took Communion in the house and there were times when Ernani asked female students to step into an adjacent room so that he could endow God's blessing on them and cleanse them of any sin. He was never locked away with them for long, but one woman who had followed him into the room told of how he had embraced her and told her that God would follow her. A little scared, she had made her exit, uncertain whether the Italian was working under God's direction or whether he was being driven by the urges of man.

The humble mechanic from the mountains was now well on his way to becoming a successful businessman, partly through the mechanic's workshop he had started – which had expanded to become a car dealership – and partly through other ventures. With his family contacts back in Pescosansonesco, he began importing cheese and olive oil, so that he was able to offer jobs as sales people to some of his most faithful followers.

As his fortunes grew, so did Ernani's dream. He was now convinced that he could, indeed, build that 'castle' he'd dreamed of back in his village. Except that it wouldn't be a castle, as such – just a magnificent country house and restaurant which would form the apex of a vast property empire. It was ambitious, he knew, but Ernani now believed enough in himself to know that it was possible.

Nothing is easy, however. And first there was the little problem of the police to be dealt with. They came knocking at the door of his dealership to check engine numbers on cars and found that some of them were on their list of stolen vehicles. Hoping that word would not get around, he appeared in court in 1990, charged with dealing in stolen cars and was given an 11-month suspended sentence. Any more problems with the law, he was warned, and he'd end up behind bars.

Ernani decided that he would have to accrue his finances with greater care, and the easiest way, as he had already found, was to entice people to hand their money over to him by doing nothing more than introducing peace, harmony and spiritual enlightenment into their lives.

There was another way, too, he realized, to earn money through the kindness of strangers. With the aid of those people who were already under his spell and considered him somewhat of a guru, he began running a series of newspaper advertisements calling for donations to a number of charities. The money came in and some of it did, indeed, trickle through to needy organizations. But large amounts are also alleged to have ended up in Ernani's bank accounts. In fact, he was getting so much money in direct donations from   followers, who wanted to help him expand his good works, and from the public who had money to spare for charities, that Ernani decided he needed to find someone to look after the books ... someone who understood that sometimes a little creative accounting was necessary in order to do God's work on Earth. He needed someone smart but with 'an edge' – and it would be all the better if his new employee had charisma, like himself, which could be used to increase his flock.

At a party in Zurich, surrounded by some of his following, he saw the man across the room. A tall man, with such an easy manner about him, a man who also had drawn many lovely women to him. They appeared to be enamoured of him. He could hardly hold back his smile as he introduced himself to the man called Helg Russak, when he discovered that the young man worked for Credit Suisse, so knew something about money.

The two men struck up a good relationship from the start and after that party a number of private meetings followed. Very carefully, Ernani sounded out his new-found friend. Helg was a good listener – his younger sister had fallen in with a religious group and he had witnessed firsthand how calm she had become. Money wasn't always easy to accrue for an older man, Ernani told his younger listener and sometimes people had to be pushed, even manipulated a little, in order for Ernani to achieve the greater good.

Over the months that Ernani Barretta spent working on Helg, the Swiss man is thought to have fallen deeply under his spell. Whatever Ernani wanted him to do, in order to expand his religious flock, he would agree to. '*He is the Maestro of my life,*' Helg was to confide to a friend. '*When I am in his presence, I know that God exists.*'

At the Maestro's bidding Helg is believed to have worked his charm on a married woman who was on the fringe of Ernani's unnamed sect, enticing her into his bed and encouraging her to make a considerable donation to his friend so that God's work could continue. The Italian was delighted. This was how it was going to be. Helg could be God's – and his – breadwinner. But Helg had also fallen in love with a member of the sect, a dark-haired Swiss girl with the soft features reminiscent of the portraits of the Renaissance Madonnas. Her name was Gabriele Franziska Sgarbi and Helg asked her to marry him.

Ernani was both pleased and perturbed – pleased that he had brought together two members of his sect, but worried that marriage would disrupt the plans that he had for his new suave apprentice. Quite simply, he wanted Helg to be free to use his charm to bed beautiful women and extract their money from them. Perhaps though, even as a married man, he could continue to meet others …

After meetings long into the night, the two men agreed that Helg would need a new identity – or rather a second identity – so that he could chop and change as the situation demanded.

'*Don't try [to do] it through a man – use your charm on a female clerk somewhere,*' Ernani told him. '*She'll do it for you. They'll all do anything for you.*'

A few days later, Helg called in at the municipal office in Dägerlen, which falls within the Winterthur district, to enquire about wedding formalities, but police were to suspect later that this was his way of sounding out who worked there. He was introduced to parish clerk Brigitta Leutenegger who was impressed by the caller's immaculate appearance. He dressed like a gentleman of the 'old school', she thought. While asking about the paperwork that would be required for a wedding, he stated that he was in the hotel business, but not any old hotel business – he claimed he built and sold luxury hotels and resorts all around the world.

The following day he was back at the municipal office. Standing in front of Brigitta's desk, he held a large bunch of flowers. As he handed them over to her, he asked if she would be able to provide him with a new identity card. Whatever was behind the request, whether he was suggesting that he wanted it in a different name, she saw the flowers as a blatant bribe and told him she couldn't help him. His smile immediately faded and he became angry, storming from the office.

But that was not the last that she was to see of him. As she left work later that day Brigitta saw him sitting outside the building in his olive-coloured Mercedes. He began to follow her. It was some 12km (7 miles) later that she was finally able to lose him. The experience left her severely shaken and was also an example of the fact that beneath Helg's charm lay something else altogether.

In the months leading up to his wedding to Gabriele in August 2001, Ernani sent Helg off on a mission ... to trawl the best hotels in the region to see if he could befriend women who were complete strangers and encourage *them* to pay *him* to bed them. Helg proved to be a great success and Ernani's bank account swelled.

The two men then set about looking for a bigger fish – a suitable rich, lonely widow with hopefully more money than sense. One name jumped out at them. Ernani had already done his homework, it seemed. He produced an old copy of a German magazine story about an aging comtesse living in the South of France.

His eyes gleamed as he read out the sentence: '*She wears diamonds as big as strawberries.*'

SEDUCTION OF A COMTESSE

The Hotel de Paris lies in the heart of Monte Carlo, the French Riviera's playground of the rich and famous. They arrive from around the world to play the casinos, sail their luxury yachts, dine in opulent surroundings and splash their money about. Beautiful women – princesses, film stars, debutantes – stroll along the marinas or lounge in pavement cafés in their designer clothes. With its ancient buildings and fabulous setting in the Mediterranean sun, it is a film producer's dream, reflected in films such as *Monte Carlo* (1930), starring Jack Buchanan and Jeanette MacDonald, and in more recent times the James Bond movies *Never Say Never Again* (1983) and *Goldeneye* (1995), in which Pierce Brosnan as Bond is seen entering the casino itself. The casino was also the setting for Ian Fleming's first 007 novel, introducing Bond, *Casino Royale*.

Many tourists spend their vacations there doing little more than 'celebrity spotting', hoping perhaps to snap a photo of someone they think they recognize stepping from a bright red Lamborghini or even heading up the steps into the Hotel de Paris, established in 1864 by Charles III of Monaco. The palace-style hotel is, after all, perfectly located for such pastimes, situated as it is next to the casino where tens of millions of dollars are won – or lost – each week.

The tall, bespectacled man who hurried up the steps to the hotel in May 2001, was not in town to look for movie stars or play the tables at the casino. Dressed in a dark suit, blue shirt and red tie, he gave the appearance of a wealthy businessman – for it was only the wealthy who could afford to check into the Hotel de Paris at a minimum rate of US $500 a night and where the guest list reads like a 'Who's Who' of the world's most affluent people.

SEDUCTION OF A COMTESSE

Security men discreetly watched him as he signed his name: *Helg Russak*. As he waited for the check-in formalities to be completed, he cast his eyes around the foyer of what is often described as the old world's first and most grand hotel, a temporary home to royalty and the biggest names in politics, entertainment and sport.

He wondered if he would spot her as the bellhop escorted him to the elevator. He knew what she looked like, for he and Ernani Barretta had spent weeks reading every word that they could find about her. He had spent hours studying her photograph in the magazines. Yes, he would know her right away should the Comtesse Verena Grafin du Pasquier-Geubels appear in the opulent foyer, but that would have been expecting too much so soon. In any case, he had to keep to the plan. They had worked it all out.

That evening, immaculately dressed in suit and tie – as the rules demanded – Helg flashed his 'Carte d'Or', provided to hotel guests for admission to private areas of the hotel and its surroundings, and strolled around the tables of the casino, gazing up at the chandeliers, the stained glass windows and sculptures, while listening to the gentle whirr of the roulette wheels. Others might have noticed him smiling, for he had also done his homework about the casino and had read how 135 years earlier a player called Charles Wells had earned himself the title of the 'man who broke the bank at Monte Carlo'. He had cleaned out the roulette table on the first two of his three visits to the principality. Tempting though it was, Helg Russak, knew he wasn't there to play the tables. Depending on his natural skills – his charm, his looks, his 'good intentions' – his winnings would come from the woman who lived as a permanent resident in the majestic hotel building next door.

The Swiss Comtesse Verena was 83 years old at the time and she had lived in the hotel as a permanent resident for the past 30 years. She was, as Ernani Barretta had said to Helg months before, quite simply 'loaded'. But she had other 'qualities' that appealed to the two men – she was lonely and liked to drink. She occupied no less than three suites, at a cost of 11,000 euros a night, but that was easily covered by the interest from the fortune lying in her bank account.

From the lounge room of one of her lavishly-appointed quarters the Comtesse would sit in a regency-style chair and gaze out across the yacht marina and the Mediterranean – one of the best views in the world. It was here that she had entertained so many of her high society friends, among them Prince Rainier of Monaco himself.

She was frequently seen dining in one of the hotel's three restaurants – *Le Louis XV* was her favourite – with friends she trusted, among them other wealthy permanent hotel residents. It all went on her bill, but then she could afford it, although she cared not so much about the money that she possessed as her jewellery, held in a bank safe deposit box and also in a secure area of the hotel. The need for security had been impressed upon her many times by her elderly friends, particularly after an apartment she kept in Paris had been broken into.

'*Oh, nobody's going to steal anything from me here,*' she told her close friend, Margrith, a frequent visitor to the Comtesse's suite. '*The hotel has fantastic security. There are security men everywhere and you wouldn't know who they are. No-one's going to walk out of here with any of my possessions. Just let them try!*'

She enjoyed the company of her close friends, but at times she would put on a colourful dress and sit in her suite alone with her memories, glancing with a soft smile at the gilt-framed photographs of loved ones from another time, another place. On special occasions, and sometimes on quite ordinary days, she brought out her pearls and wore them in a long single string around her neck. Gold and diamond rings adorned her fingers and she would rarely be seen without pearl or ruby earrings. One of her diamonds, she confided to friends, was worth over 300,000 euros.

She had once been a beautiful woman in her younger days, a time when she had married twice, picked up a fortune and earned herself a noble title and a double-barrelled name. Despite her advancing years, she clung to the past, refusing to accept the inevitable approach of old age. She dyed her hair, dark blonde, then red to hide the grey; wore designer clothes, specially made for her, and on colder days when she stepped out to walk along the seafront she would wrap herself in thick, genuine furs.

SEDUCTION OF A COMTESSE

Each year, at the most important event in Monaco's social calendar – the Rose Ball – the Comtesse was invited as a VIP guest and she would occupy the same table as the principality's royal family. The best champagne was poured and the signatures of international celebrities were scribbled on to cheques, the proceeds awarded to the Princess Grace Foundation to help disadvantaged children. Comtesse Verena was among the most generous donors.

In fact her benevolence knew no boundaries, as long as the gift was for a good cause – she even donated funds for a memorial to a 'new' saint, Padre Pio, who is said to have overcome physical and spiritual attacks by the devil and remained devoted to God until his death in 1968, after which he was venerated as a saint in the Catholic Church.

As for her own death, when it came, she wanted it to happen in the style to which she had for so long been accustomed. '*I'll be happy to die in one of two ways,*' she told her friends with a chuckle. '*It should be in a fatal crash in a Rolls Royce, or in a plane crash when I'm flying first class. It doesn't really matter which, but I must be comfortable at the time.*'

If the aging Comtesse could not be found in the hotel's dining room she might be found in the Bar American, listening to the piano player while enjoying a fine malt whisky, her favourite tipple.

Helg watched her for days as she went about her lonely routine, shuffling as she did at times, with the aid of a stick, through the foyer to either the restaurant or the bar. Some days he just ambled along behind her as she took a walk along the waterfront, noting the people who she bade good day to, reading her habits. The more he knew about her, the easier it would be to hook her. Watching her in the restaurant he saw that she had no dislikes on the menu. She liked chocolate. She was happy to exchange greetings with strangers as long as they showed her respect; she seemed to expect that. She was sprightly, had her wits about her.

Yes, softly, softly, that was the way, just as he and Ernani had agreed.

Finally, it was time. She was alone in the bar. He made his way to the Comtesse's table. An innocent question about the hotel, its famous guests of the past. That would start it …

SEDUCTION OF A COMTESSE

On the afternoon of 26 May, Dr Christina Weyer and her multi-millionaire husband, Consul Hans Hermann, a trader in nobility and academic titles, were sitting on the sun deck. She was drinking camomile tea, her husband a diet soft drink. The Hotel de Paris was a home away from home for the jet-setting couple, who had been married for 11 years, much of that time spent in Rio de Janeiro, although on more recent occasions they could be found in Monte Carlo, Nice or Zurich. The Consul joked to his friends that he remained super-fit because his wife, the doctor, made sure he remained healthy.

Among their friends they included the grand Comtesse, but on that particular day they were watching a man swimming lengths of the pool, as she rested in her suite. The Consul, in particular, was impressed – he thought he was fit, with the constitution of a man 20 years younger, but the guest in the pool was like a fish. He and his wife were awe-struck at his speed and his power and thought perhaps, in all seriousness, they were watching an Olympian.

The next minute Helg Russak clambered out of the pool and, casually passing the couple as he wiped himself down, gave them a greeting. An hello from one guest to another. The couple exchanged pleasantries – it was easy enough for the Weyers to make conversation by simply commenting on his swimming ability. They did not realize that it was he who was subtly leading the conversation. Then the three of them found a new and more intimate topic when he mentioned he had learned to swim when he was living in Rio, where he had been born. He even broke into a bit of Portuguese, either to impress them or to prove what he had said, but it wasn't necessary. Their faces had already lit up at the mention of Rio. Why, they had spent many years there themselves! As easy as that, he had them.

Later, the Weyers caught up with their friend the Comtesse. She was in an exceptionally good mood. She had met a charming young man in the bar, a lawyer by the name of Alexandre. He had told her he was chairman of the legal firm of Russak Society and Partners, whose headquarters were in New York. She and Alexandre were having dinner that very evening, said the Comtesse, adding to her friends: '*Why don't you both come and join us? I'd love you to meet him.*'

The Comtesse and her new friend were already at the table when the Weyers arrived. To their great surprise the dinner guest was none other than the 'Olympic swimmer', who jumped to his feet to greet them. He was smartly dressed in a suit and tie (but who would dine any other way in the Hotel de Paris?) and was now wearing spectacles.

Christina thought his manners both in greeting them and at the table were impeccable, but as the wine flowed and the group chatted about their fine surroundings and the weather, she noticed that he said very little about himself. He preferred to listen to the chatter of the other three at the table, although when appropriate he went out of his way to pass on a compliment. How well the Comtesse looked … he was sure she would go on living for ever … and the Consul, his wife was obviously keeping a good eye on him for him to be in such good shape … and Christina, if a typical lady for such a fine hotel could be found in the whole of Monaco, it must surely be her – she just seemed to fit in so well with her surroundings. They were all overwhelmed by his compliments and his modesty.

The following day three roses arrived in Comtesse Verena's suite, from 'Alexandre', along with a note to say how much he had enjoyed her company and that perhaps they could meet again if she felt so inclined.

Flattered by the attentions of a man young enough to be her grandson, she did agree to meet him again. The flowers, her friends were to reflect much later, when it was far too late, were a very clever ploy – the work of a master of his trade. Three single roses touched the heart more deeply than a big bunch of flowers. The simple roses were far more romantic, implying that they had been chosen personally by the sender.

Over an intimate dinner between just the two of them this time, Helg told the Comtesse how impressed he was by her outlook on life – how she refused to allow a few extra years to interfere with the fun that she was obviously having. They were words that the Comtesse had never heard before from someone so much younger than herself. She reached out her hand to grasp his and thank him for his kindness. The following day, chocolates arrived with another tender note from the new, charming man who was insinuating himself into her life.

The Weyers were astonished to learn that within days Alexandre, who they came across in the foyer or at the pool from time to time – and once had politely helped them carry their shopping bags to their suite – had moved in to the Comtesse's quarters.

'*Is it really true?*' Christina asked the Comtesse. '*Alexandre has actually moved in with you?*'

Her smile was answer enough, but she added: '*We're in love, you know. We're going to get married.*'

Christina and her husband were both amazed and alarmed. While they had suspected that the Comtesse was lonely, despite the friends who surrounded her, they found it impossible to believe that she could really have fallen in love with a man so much younger than herself – and that he, who appeared to have all the qualities that would win the heart of any woman of his age, should have been smitten by an octogenarian widow who needed a walking stick to get about, dyed her hair to hide the white and who wore false teeth.

'*Are you sure about this?*' Christina and the Consul asked the Comtesse in as tactful a manner as they could muster.

'*Oh yes, I'm quite sure,*' she replied in a slightly dismissive tone. '*We've already arranged to buy our wedding rings. You see, I know he loves me and I love him.*'

They were no ordinary wedding rings, of course – the couple went to the Monte Carlo outlet of Graff, the world-renowned diamond jewellery house, the first choice of the ultra-wealthy, royalty and celebrities. Together the elderly widow and her 'fiancé', the clever young lawyer, who had introduced himself as Alexandre, perused the offerings. Graff rings are made from the finest quality white diamonds, which are then set in white gold. But that wasn't enough for the Comtesse, who was not expecting any change from 36,000 euros for the ring which she bought for herself – she also ordered a signet ring for Helg, and asked for her coat of arms to be emblazened on it. How well it would match the gold US $4,000 Rolex Cellini watch that she had already bought for him. They headed back to the hotel, the Comtesse all smiles. But her smile did not go anywhere near matching Helg's grin. Ernani Barretta would be well pleased with his ongoing work, he thought – he had told him as much in frequent phone call updates between them.

The truth was, Helg had already been in action in the weeks before he slithered into the high-class world of Comtesse Verena. He had befriended a British millionairess, who lived in London but who owned an apartment in Cannes, 50km (31 miles) along the coast. Just as only Helg and the Comtesse knew what went on behind the closed doors of her suite, only he and the millionairess could account for what went on between them. Whatever happened, she was to insist to the police later that details of her relationship with Helg Russak were to remain strictly confidential.

The Comtesse told her close friend, Margrith, a stylish woman, 20 years younger than herself, about her intention to marry Helg. Margrith was also shocked and urged her not to proceed with such foolishness. Why, Verena knew nothing about the man and the 47-year-age gap was quite ridiculous. But the Comtesse insisted, pulling out photographs that had been taken of her and Helg together. There was a picture of the Comtesse, her hair dyed red, sitting on a couch in a pink floral dress, wearing her long pearl necklace, and Helg, in a business-like white shirt and a polka-dot tie, with his arm wrapped around her. There was great happiness on her face, while he wore a boyish grin.

'*Can't you see the delight in his eyes?*' she asked Margrith. '*You can see that he really loves me – as I do him. And Margrith, I'd like to ask you, please, to help with the wedding preparations.*'

Reluctantly Margrith agreed to do as her friend asked. She believed there was no point in protesting further. She had tried to talk Verena out of it but the Comtesse's mind was set.

Verena wanted to look her very best – and youngest – for the new man in her life, so she called Paul, her hairdresser and asked him to dye her hair a fiery red, much brighter than the tint she had used before to hide the grey. She couldn't wait to give him the reason. Plans for her wedding, her third, were proceeding without a hitch, she revealed. Like her other friends, Paul was astonished when he learned the age of her groom-to-be: 36. She was blinded by love, he thought, and anything he might dare to say would prove pointless.

However, it soon became even more apparent to the suspicious Christina Weyer and her husband that the charming man whose arm Comtesse Verena now clung to so possessively as they strolled along the waterfront, was up to no good. They decided to check him out and with careful questioning they heard him tell them that he owned an apartment in Cannes, one that he was intending to sell. They managed to find out the address from him and drove along the coast to look at it. They were astonished to find a bedsheet hanging from the balcony with the words 'For Sale' on it, along with his mobile phone number. The couple also found out that the apartment was not 'Alexandre's' but belonged to a wealthy English woman – Helg's millionairess.

'*Don't go ahead with this marriage*,' the Weyers begged the Comtesse. '*We think he's tricking you.*'

But the Comtesse would hear nothing against her young fiancé. In any case, she was preparing to help him financially to prepare their future together. He wanted to buy a house for them but his funds were tied up and he needed cash to start things off. Comtesse Verena had many of her enormous funds deposited in an account in the tiny principality of Liechtenstein, referring to it jokingly as 'Frankenstein', where she had also spent a lot of money. But she had transferred 360,000 euros to the Hotel de Paris years before because she had found that there could be problems in getting large sums of money transferred from one country to another.

Within a short time, several wads of cash were being stuffed into Helg Russak's suitcase. He wasn't going to risk transferring it through any bank system to Ernani. Much safer to drive back to Switzerland or to Italy – wherever Ernani instructed – and hand it over personally.

As he continued to woo her, wining and dining in the finest restaurants Monte Carlo could offer – with her money being used to settle the bills – Helg asked Verena about her chateau on the shores of

SEDUCTION OF A COMTESSE

Lake Geneva, which he wondered might be a good place for them to spend their honeymoon. The Comtesse was enchanted by the suggestion and his enthusiasm and, as the wedding was still several months away, she agreed to his plan that they pay the villa a visit.

No-one gave the couple a second glance as they approached the check-in desk at the swish Hotel du Rhone on the right bank of the River Rhone, a few minutes from Geneva's financial heart, its galleries and shops. The staff and guests might well have assumed that the pair were a grandmother and grandson – even when they moved into a suite together with a view over the river. Helg had wanted her there because this was where she had a bank account and had easy access to her money – more importantly, she was far away from that sceptical and interfering couple, the Weyers.

After visiting her villa and enjoying a tour around the fringes of the largest lake in Central Europe, taking tea in small towns and stopping at vineyards, Helg began to apply the screws.

He had a grave problem, he finally confessed to the Comtesse, and unless it went away, he might not be able to marry her – nor might he live to see his next birthday. He promised to tell her more later. As they dined in the hotel one evening, he hesitatingly recounted a story that had its origins in the United States, where his legal company was located.

One day, he told the Comtesse, he had been involved in a road accident, knocking down a child who had run out in front of him. The little girl was rushed to hospital in a critical state. She survived, but she would require years of ongoing treatment. Her family were demanding compensation from him, well beyond that which his insurance company was willing to pay.

As the Comtesse listened in growing horror, Helg claimed that the girl's family was headed by none other than a major Mafia figure and that they wanted several thousands of dollars from him in compensation. And time was running out. He didn't have to spell out that the Mafia had more than a few connections in Europe. He had paid what he could, but his funds had dried up and there was money still owing.

He played it well. Shook his head at his plight. Acted superbly like the innocent caught up in a nightmare beyond his control. She gazed at his boyish face. This young man who had made her so happy had kept this personal torment from her, knowing how it would upset her and how it might be misconstrued by others. She admired the courage of her handsome companion, her fiancé – and yes, of course she would help him.

'*How much do you need?*' she asked.

He shook his head again, a gesture that suggested he dare not even mention it.

She asked him again: '*Alexandre … you must tell me – how much?*'

This was it. '*Another US $2 million.*'

Did she gasp? He couldn't be sure but if she did it wasn't because she didn't have it – rather it would have been because she realized what a terrible fix he was in.

'*I will help you,*' she said. '*Tomorrow we shall go to the bank.*'

And they did.

She drew it out in Swiss francs, hundreds of thousands of them, all in cash. With feigned reluctance written all over his face, his hands reached out to take the money.

They remained in the hotel. There are suggestions that, to avoid raising the Comtesse's suspicions, the money was collected by a member of Ernani Barretta's sect and taken to Zurich, just 225km (140 miles) away. Helg knew that he had the old lady in the palm of his hand, so anxious was she to do anything for love and affection, and he set into motion stage two of the plan – something that would involve cleaning her out of everything, if not now, then in a very short time …

The Comtesse had revealed to him that she had an adopted son, who would inherit her wealth on her death. But he had a drinking problem and had already squandered a great deal of her money. This was music to Helg's ears. Now, with US $2 million already extracted from his gullible target, he had a new proposal to put to her: sign over all her assets to him. She would know then, that all her money, her belongings, were safe. Even a long way into the future – his discreet way of mentioning her eventual death – was it not better that he, her husband-to-be, should be in control, rather than a relative who would waste it all?

He watched her eyes as she sat back in her chair, contemplatively.

And, he suggested, as a lawyer and a former banker, he would be able to control all her finances. Invest them on the money market. She would not have to worry any more about reckless relatives or knaves who might be after her money. They would, they both agreed, have to make out a formal agreement and then he would take care of her entire estate. It was impossible to disagree with him and if Ernani Barretta could have been watching the scene he would have congratulated himself for having chosen such an impressive disciple so well.

On 12 July, Comtesse Verena walked into the Geneva office of a notary public and made all the arrangements to place 27.9 million euros into the care of her fiancé. A doctor's certificate was presented, confirming that she was in control of her faculties and was mentally alert. Within a few days the money was transferred from the Comtesse's account in Liechtenstein to two Swiss bank accounts held by Helg Russak.

They remained in Geneva, the Comtesse talking excitedly about the wedding, which would take place in a few months. He showed good faith by paying her bills – with her own money, to which he now had total access. It was true what he had told her – that he knew how to handle large sums of money competently. He simply left out that this time around it would be for himself and his friend, Ernani Barretta.

At the end of July he told Verena that a business matter had come up. He had to fly to Rio and he would be away for several weeks. She was not to worry. He reassured her that the wedding was still on.

How true that was. But his bride was not to be Comtesse Verena Grafin du Pasquier-Geubels.

'MONEY IS SIN – AND WOMEN MUST BE CLEANSED OF IT'

It was a wedding fit for a king and queen, for it took place in the fabulous Abbazia di San Clemente – San Clemente Abbey – just a few kilometres from Ernani's village of Pescosansonesco. It was ironic that the mediaeval abbey, located beside the ancient road leading from the east coast of Italy to Naples, had become a great wealth accumulator. As the 100 or so guests, most of them faithful members of Ernani Barretta's growing sect, gathered to watch the couple exchange vows before a priest on that sunny day on 5 August 2001, sculpted stone figures, including those of abbots and demons, gazed down at them. There were some fearful creatures among them, winged monsters gnawing into the necks of monks; others fought among themselves.

The church and its monastery had been founded by Emperor Ludovico II in AD 871, when it was dedicated to the Holy Trinity. In the following year, the remains of San Clemente, a martyr Pope from the late 1st century, were given to the monastery by Pope Adriano II. Clemente, according to the story passed down through the centuries, had been banished by the Emperor Trajan and he was eventually killed by being tied to an anchor and tossed into the sea. His bones were recovered and carried to Rome, before they were brought on the journey into the hills to lie in the abbey. Whether the guests who gathered at the wedding of Helg Russak and his young Swiss bride knew, or even cared, about the history of the abbey was of little consequence as Ernani spoke to the guests about his vision for the future – he would build a grand sanctuary for his own disciples, a place in Pescosansonesco where they could meditate, just like the abbots of old, and find peace with their maker.

Helg and his bride, Gabriele Sgarbi, accompanied by Ernani, strolled among the towering arches of the main church after the ceremony, staring up at a huge stone pulpit from the 12th century and stopping to look at the marble casket where the bones of San Clemente were said to lie. A casual visitor watching them might have considered there was a religious aura surrounding the three but the wickedness of the heart cannot be seen.

Ernani and the newly-weds travelled back to his old village, where he had run through the streets as a hungry child, never imagining that some 50 years later he would return with a fabulous plan to erect the grandest building in the region. Yet despite the millions that Helg had already accrued, the Italian was determined to pull in even more money and over the next few days, before the guests dispersed, he implored them all to work hard at saving so that they could give generously to his spiritual cause, a sanctuary that would be a centre for true believers. They would be able to stay, rest and pray.

Helg and his bride spent a short honeymoon on the Adriatic coast where he explained that he would soon have to travel to the south of France because he had financial matters to attend to, although it is thought that he did not go into any fine detail about the Comtesse. However, it was to be claimed by police sources much later on that Gabriele was already aware of the unique way in which her new husband planned to expand the family coffers.

As he planned his return to the South of France, others were examining his relationship with the elderly Comtesse in detail: Dr Christina Weyer and her husband, the Consul, having phoned their friend several times and learned that she had placed all her assets in the control of the man she constantly referred to as her fiancé, were determined that the wedding had to be stopped at all costs. That was, if there *ever* was going to be a wedding – of that they both had their doubts. They wondered, in fact, whether Alexandre Russak, or whatever his name was – for they could not be sure about anything that he had said about himself – would ever be seen again.

By now, Verena had returned to Monte Carlo from Switzerland to wait for the return of her husband-to-be. The Weyers didn't wait any longer. They went to the police headquarters there where they found a number of officers who knew the Comtesse and who were truly shocked at hearing about the stranger who, in a flash, had extracted millions from her and had now taken control of all her assets.

The police believed they had a good enough case to charge Russak with fraud, at least. But he was not in France. The co-operation of the police in Switzerland, Germany, Austria and Italy – the most likely places that he might be – was sought. The hunt was on.

The Comtesse was devastated at being informed by the police that her fiancé was a charlatan. She refused at first to believe that Alexandre was not her fiance's real name and that he was a con man. He had treated her so well, after all. He had paid for everything, admittedly with her *own* money, but he had made sure that all the financial pressures she had experienced were taken from her. Her many weeks with him had been the best she had had in years. He had given her new life, a cause for living on until, well, until she was 100! But gradually the police along with her friends the Weyers convinced her that her fiancé was indeed a crook. She was advised to sit tight and allow the police get on with their work.

Remaining in touch with the police, the Weyers heard more stories about the man whose name they had now found out was Helg, not Alexandre, Russak. He had told the truth when he informed the Comtesse that he was a banker, but what he had failed to tell her was that he had won the hearts of other women along the Mediterranean coast and had dipped his fingers into their purses as well.

Her fiancé, her 'wonderful young man', it emerged was little more than a gigolo. He was paid for sex – although the women he conquered did not realize that when they 'loaned' him money to help him out of a spot of bother which he confessed to them he had with the Mafia after knocking over a child in America. These women were paying him for their temporary enjoyment. There were times, the Weyers learned, when he had threatened the women who asked for their money back that he would tell their husbands or their families what they had been up to. So, a blackmailer *and* a gigolo.

He was good at it. Very good, it seemed. The best. And Ernani Barretta was very pleased with him as he counted up the fortune he was steadily accruing. He began to make plans to extend his motor business in Zurich, but he ran foul of the authorities for violating zoning rules and that, along with his earlier suspended sentence for dealing in stolen cars, resulted in him being thrown into jail for two months. He considered it a minor interruption to his dreams of an international empire with followers from around the world.

But where was Helg Russak in all this?

Police forces in France, Germany, Austria, Switzerland and Italy were looking for him, following the complaints that the Weyers had made on behalf of the Comtesse. She was still in two minds about her young man … whether he was being unfairly maligned without having had the chance to exonerate himself, or whether he was, in fact, a charming villain.

The police finally caught up with him in Lausanne, 170km (106 miles) from Zurich. He claimed that his name was not Russak, but Sgarbi – the maiden name of his wife Gabriele. Officials were not put off and they threw the book at him, charging him with grand theft in relation to the Comtesse. They warned him that if he had gone ahead with the marriage to the old lady he would have been charged with bigamy, too.

'*This is ridiculous,*' he protested. '*I'm in love with Verena and she loves me. If I have money, it's what women like to give me. Verena gave to me willingly. There is no ulterior motive. Never before in my life have I met someone who means so much to me. Our feelings were mutual. Our lives were about to change to something more wonderful than either of us have ever experienced.*'

He was charged all the same.

'*They've got him,*' the Weyers told the Comtesse. '*Now he'll go to jail.*'

'*No, no, I don't want that,*' she immediately exclaimed, for the truth was Helg Russak, as she now knew him, had breathed life into her old bones. If she could just get her money and her assets back, all would be forgiven. Even so, she agreed under pressure from her friends to proceed with the charges, for without her agreement the authorities would not be able to bring him to court.

He had spent eight days in jail on remand before he was eventually brought into the courtroom and led to the dock. He gazed about him.

'MONEY IS SIN – AND WOMEN MUST BE CLEANSED OF IT'

The Comtesse was present with her head down for the most part. Occasionally she lifted it as the court officials prepared to present the damning evidence they had against the prisoner. Helg caught her eye. What she saw, she was to tell her friends later, was a sad young man who had brought so much happiness into her life and who had been consumed by the lifestyle she, in turn, had been able to provide to him. She even saw herself as being partly to blame for his dilemma. She had fed his dreams of a better life and responsibility for that hung heavily on her shoulders.

His glance at her across the courtroom told her that he still loved her, she told her friend Margrith later. She heard his unspoken plea, begging her not to go ahead with this. It would ruin his life – an unfair return for all the enjoyment he had brought to her. And now she was hearing that he was willing to do everything he could to return the money to her, even though its use would have been for her benefit.

Biting her lip, the Comtesse told the court: '*I do not wish to proceed.*'

Her friends told her she was crazy to let him off the hook, but she said his promise to return the money evened everything up. She needed a lawyer to handle the negotiations and the legal firm did not come cheap – a reported 490,000 euros. And then there were the funds that Helg said had gone on 'their expenses' and could not be recouped. Finally, it was agreed he would refund 25.4 million francs (16,600,000 euro) out of a total of 30.55 million francs (20,051,000 euro) that he had extracted from her. Even if he had genuinely spent a couple of million euros with the Comtesse, travelling, dining, staying in the best hotels, there were still two million euros unaccounted for – but he was off the hook.

The experience had shaken Comtesse Verena. Although she had forgiven him, as the weeks went by and her friends insisted she had had a very narrow escape and that if Helg had not been caught she would have lost everything, she accepted that a need for the companionship of a man who loved her had turned her head.

'*I couldn't bear to see him in prison, but yes, of course, I'm very upset by suggestions that he was only after me for my money,*' she told her close circle of friends as they gathered to comfort her in her suite. They were concerned at how ill she looked, realizing that as time went by the deceit was having a growing impact on her health.

'He told me he loved me and would be with me for ever, until my death,' she said. There was no bitterness in her voice, however; just disappointment. *'I never wanted to lose him. I loved him. But I hope that now he has returned most of the money we can remain friends.'*

It was not to be. She never saw him again, although a member of Ernani's sect was to claim later that he made an attempt to see the Comtesse when her health declined.

While there was no evidence that his betrayal was the cause, Comtesse Verena grew weaker. Her friends thought that she was physically shrinking before them, all in a matter of months. She was not so careful with her makeup and there were days when she did not even bother to put it on – such a contrast to the proud old lady who would never dare to step out of her suite without dressing with great care. She slid into months of illness and bewilderment before being moved to a Swiss clinic, where she lingered on in distress before passing away. It was just a year after Helg Russak had come into her life. Her friends believed that she had died of a broken heart, her last-ever chance of love shattered.

But whether he cared or not, Helg Russak was no more. He had now begun calling himself *Helg Sgarbi*, for he knew that after his narrow escape from what would have been a long prison sentence he was in police files in a number of countries and they were probably watching out for him.

Despite this, he remained devoted to Ernani Barretta. The Italian had such a strong influence over him that he was determined to give him everything he earned from the women he could seduce, for Ernani's dream had not faded – to bring God to the masses – and a little something for himself, as well. And Helg was determined to help him in every way he could. Just how he had become so influenced by a once-struggling car mechanic from a poor Italian village, the name of which few people had heard of, let alone being able to pronounce, was to baffle psychologists in years to come. But there were many other aspects of Helg's life that were to become the focus of lively discussions among all manner of the experts who study and dissect the mind. There was, they were all to agree, a kind of pecking order – Ernani needed Helg; Helg needed rich and lonely women; and the women needed Helg's love and affection, false as it was.

The simple answer, it seemed – if the psychologists had ever learned of it – were the words that Ernani whispered into Helg's ear shortly after they met: '*Money is sin and women who have it must be cleansed of it. It must be returned to the Lord and I am his servant.*'

Helg continued his romantic reconnoitres, trawling the swanky hotels of Europe, artfully watching any woman he saw sitting alone in a bar or restaurant, checking out her jewellery, for unless it looked expensive – and his trained eye could pick it – he would not bother to move in. Satisfied that a potential catch would be worth approaching, he used any number of the pick-up lines in his vocabulary. Sometimes it took a day or two, on other occasions it might be a week or so, but once his victims were hooked the 'borrowing' began. Some of his catches, police suspected, were too embarrassed to file a report – particularly if they had gone to bed with him and they were married. Often it was just a hint of the consequences should a husband learn about his wife's infidelity – and her financial generosity – that was enough to bring them to heel. It was smooth sailing. Love, money, a threat … And he was very careful this time. Any suggestion that the woman involved might be trouble and he was off.

But while he was doing the rounds, improving his art of seduction, Dr Christina Weyer and her Consul husband Hans-Hermann were digging into his background, pulling together information gleaned from sympathetic police officers. There was a religious sect and money that the Swiss man was extorting was pouring into it. They had heard, too, that one of Helg's victims had sought psychiatric treatment after becoming trapped in his 'pay or I'll tell' net. What was more, Christina believed that he had also targeted her while he was staying at the Hotel de Paris, should his seduction of the Comtesse fail. Christina was blonde, attractive and very wealthy – just his type.

The more they thought about it, the more they were convinced that he knew exactly who they were and had set up the swimming pool meeting at the hotel well in advance. Not only had he spoken of his life in Rio, knowing that they had also lived there, but he had also mentioned that he had previously worked at Credit Suisse – their bank. Had he used his old contacts in the bank to find out about the Weyers? They had no real evidence of that, but piecing together everything that they had discovered about him they were convinced that he was preparing to move in on either Christina or the Comtesse. The Comtesse had made it easy for him, falling in love with him, so his full attention remained on her.

If only to satisfy themselves that they were doing something, albeit too late, for their dear, duped friend the Comtesse, the Weyers decided to confront him. Several months after the Comtesse's death, they traced Helg to an apartment in the Glattbrugg district of Zurich where he had set up home with his new wife, Gabriele. It was an unpleasant confrontation and shortly afterwards Christina received a terrifying letter.

'*You have interfered, uninvited, into my affairs,*' Helg wrote. '*You should consider what you are doing, because you are coming close to losing your beautiful face.*' He also told her that he was prepared to expose an alleged sexual encounter that they had had.

For a man who believed he could read people – particularly women – like a book, the letter was a grave mistake. The Weyers took it to the police.

Before they could act, however, Helg Sgarbi as he was now calling himself, was off again, wearing his 'little boy-lost' mask, which hid the face of a practiced blackmailing gigolo.

'THE MAFIA ARE EVERYWHERE'

They remark, his victims, how alike he was in looks to Julian Kaye, the male prostitute played by actor Richard Gere in the 1980 film *American Gigolo*. The movie is an ugly story of love for sale, with the women doing the paying, but it is also about violence and murder.

It was a world into which Helg Sgarbi had stepped and soon his own exploits would be on film, although there would be nothing make-believe about what he got up to. Unlike Richard Gere's gigolo, Helg Sgarbi had no pimp as such, but a 'guru' in the form of Ernani Barretta, who sent him on his missions. For the most part, Helg worked on his own initiative, seeking out vulnerable wealthy women, arousing long-lost emotions, satisfying them sexually and leading them on to feel that they were desirable, whatever their age. He was gifted, an illusionist who turned the seemingly unwanted into the coveted.

Gigolos are members of the oldest profession in the world. Their name is derived from the French '*gigolette*', meaning 'dancing girl' or, more commonly, 'prostitute'. They can be found making themselves available to women and men, young and old – as long as they are paid. They are found in every corner of the world, muscular, long-haired young men hanging around the beaches of Bali, Rio, Italy; some might sit in hotel lobbies, 'lounge lizards' in open-necked white shirts, throwing a smile to a passing female guest; or they might be well dressed in a suit and tie, sitting in a bar in London, New York or Rome and inviting single women to join them. But they are gigolos, all the same, they might approach with a flower in one hand and the other hand on their heart but they are thinking of only one thing: money.

The Comtesse Verena would have been shocked had it been spelled out to her – that her young and adorable companion, the man who she intended to marry, was nothing more than a 'callboy', as the Germans refer to gigolos, although, a 'high-class' one, at that. It might have been too much for her heart to have heard the more common expressions applied to those males who are paid for their escort services … 'man whores', 'man sluts' or, as they are referred to in the Caribbean, 'sanky-pankies'.

No, she would not have wanted to hear such things said about her beau, although in her many, luxurious years, the Comtesse would have known about gigolos, for it was common knowledge that Swiss and German women often headed abroad to Morocco, Greece and even the Dominican Republic in search of short-term romance – and were willing to pay for it. Each summer there has been an exodus of women, usually middle-aged and above, from cities around the world, to the latest sex hot spot where male escorts await them with open arms, ready to dine with them, take them to the tourist spots and share their bed – all for a fee.

These women are too overwhelmed to realize that the romantic lines that often pour from their companions' lips have been spoken time and again to others. The words are nothing more than poetic lies. But they fall for it. They even, in some cases, become emotionally attached. But they fail to realize that for the most part they are nothing more than a commodity. Smooth talk and desperation for love can come at a high emotional, financial and physical cost.

Psychiatrists have long tried to find out what makes gigolos tick, but there appears to be no common factor except that they see their clients as nothing more than mere objects, a means to have a good time, while getting paid for it.

It has been suggested that gigolos get into the game because they have been abused, sexually or physically, as children, or because they have a personality disorder. Indian psychiatrist Dr J.M. Wadhawan suggests that gigolos have a sociopathic or antisocial nature, while sex and marriage therapist Dr Vinod Chebbi believes that they feel proud of their skill at providing sexual satisfaction and, so, glorify themselves.

Does Helg Sgarbi fit into any of these patterns? He was certainly not abused as a child, but, in his threatening letter to Christina Weyer he certainly revealed sociopathic tendencies. Yet there remains Helg's devotion to the man who was allegedly driving him, Ernani Barretta.

It is perhaps simple: to Ernani, Helg was the perfect gigolo. He had the looks, the manners and an air that seemed to be saying *'I'm just a boy at heart'*. Women *wanted* to love him, to care for him, while his hand, out of sight, was feeling around in their purse and Ernani Barretta knew it. He only had to look again at his burgeoning bank account to confirm that.

★ ★ ★

November 2001
Ernani was feeling the heat from the police. Some of his disillusioned followers, incensed by his increasingly exaggerated claims that he was a messenger of God, were spreading the word that he was taking their money as 'donations for the service of Jesus' but not actually doing anything with the money. They had poured thousands of euros into his cult, as it was now known, but his promise to build a church in Italy to the glory of God had still not got underway and many now felt spiritually disillusioned.

Uplifted initially by Ernani's words, he had been able to do nothing more for them. Their lives had not changed for the better. Depressions that had faded when he had given them his blessings in the early weeks now returned with vengeance. Physical afflictions that had seemed to be healing when he'd touched them, now had returned. But while a number of Ernani's followers drifted away from his circle, others who had invested large sums in his promises remained, hoping that tomorrow, or the day after, would bring about spiritual stimulation.

Helg remained in close phone contact with his mentor, updating him with news of his latest conquest. Such liaisons were not always successful: a one-night stand, a failure to 'communicate' with the woman and hopes of any ongoing relationship were doomed. He was still eager to get his name changed officially in case the police were following him through credit card transactions and any other documentation he might use in the name of 'Russak', a second name would be most convenient.

In 2002, in the 20,000-strong community of Goldach, nestled on the shores of Lake Constance, he applied his charm once again in the registry office – and came out with a new identity. Where he had failed once before by giving a woman flowers in the municipal office in Dägerlen, he now officially took his wife's maiden name and could be known as *Helg Sgarbi*. Russak was dead – unless it became convenient to resurrect him again.

Now, back with his wife for a time, the two of them travelled to Pescosansonesco in his Mercedes, where Ernani was at last about to build his communal centre, which would also include a restaurant and a small hotel. The work had begun years earlier, but now it was to proceed in earnest. Assuring Helg that he saw him as a modern-day 'Peter', Jesus' favourite disciple and his rock, Ernani invited him to lay the cornerstone of the main building of the country house and estate. The rest of the 'disciples' who remained, those who had followed him to the village and were staying in local homes and even in tents as the building went ahead, were well and truly under Ernani's spell. As was Helg.

In time to come, they agreed that Helg, like themselves, had been brainwashed. But at that time, they believed in the man who declared himself to be 'God's messenger'. They were convinced that Ernani was working for God under 'His' directions. Ernani's claims expanded into the fanciful, however. He was not just *working* for God. He was *God's son*. He was Jesus returned. Each of the cult members who vowed to live and work in the centre as it neared completion was told that he or she was a true disciple of Jesus. Those who had donated the most money were appointed disciples with the same names as the original 12 who followed Christ.

At first, when he was calling in his flock in Zurich, Ernani believed that he would need several of his male disciples to spread out around the hotels of Europe, scamming what they could from the rich and lonely. He asked Helg to sound out a few of the 'brethren'.

One of Helg's former college friends was to recall later: '*He urged me to try it, to just go out and about, pull in the old ladies and they would pay up if you had a sad story to tell them. He told me it was dead easy. Just fill their ears with romance and take their money. I have to admit he sounded*

*so convincing. He just knew it would work for me because it had worked so well
for him. While I wanted no part of it, he left me without any doubt that it was
easy money – and could be quite pleasurable at the same time.'*

Ernani's brothers and sisters and other relatives from around the
district came by to watch his estate take shape. Soon, he told them, he
would be able to buy houses for them all. God was taking care of them
– although if Helg Sgarbi was around he might have cast a friendly eye
in his direction for there was no greater benefactor than he, not to
forget the women he had scammed.

Ernani Barretta's claims of godliness went beyond words. He told
his followers that because God had given him his personal blessing he
was now able to walk on water. On a recent trip to Egypt, he said, two
witnesses had seen him walking through the waves. God had given
him the faith to do it and he would show all his followers again one
day when they travelled to the Adriatic coast.

At night, Ernani told his disciples, he could feel Christ's pain in his
side, where the Roman soldiers had lanced the *'old Jesus'*. God had
given him the gift of transcendentation and he had travelled to the war
zones of the world and watched and felt the suffering of others.
Sometimes, he told his disciples, when they could not see him
anywhere around Pescosansonesco he was in fact still there, invisible,
watching over them. At other times, when they met a stranger in the
village, it would be him, Ernani, for it was another miracle that God
had bestowed upon him – he could enter into another body and leave
again whenever he wished.

'If you believe in God, as I do, these things will also be given to you,' he
told his mixed flock of lawyers, architects, students and laymen. They
were of all ages and of different nationalities but what they shared was
a devotion to Ernani, for only through him, he impressed on them,
could they truly touch God. At the time Ernani's disciples were all
smitten by the inexplicable power of the former car mechanic.

Many of the cult members had been encouraged to follow Ernani
by a sect member, who had since died, whom they had met in Zurich.
He had informed them that he had seen Eranani lay his hands on the
sick in the early days and within minutes the afflicted were healed. It

was Bible talk and those who heard it – mostly people who were dissatisfied with their lives and were looking for something new and profound – were deeply moved. It was little wonder that so many wanted to follow him to Pescosansonesco where stories of his miracles poured out, this time from his own lips. Sometimes he would wake and find his bed wet with blood … the suffering of Christ. The pain throughout his body was unbearable and sometimes, he told them, he would have to leave his body lying there in that bloody bed while he recreated himself and went to another place where he could rest.

He could read the minds of all his disciples, so their thoughts must remain pure. If they had doubts, he would know it, he told them. If they loved him he would know it, too, and he would love them all the more for it. He led them in prayer morning and night for he told them that there was great power in collective prayer. They must pray for more followers because they would be able to give, too, towards the erection of new buildings from which God's love could be expanded.

There were times when he was found lying on the tiled floor, a pool of blood around him. It was the blood of Christ, he said again, seeping from his own body, but no-one realized that the local butcher was making good money from Ernani, selling him pints of cows' blood.

He repeated words he had spoken so often to members of his fledgling cult in Zurich: '*In years past, it was your parents who gave you love and taught you. Now I will be the one. Listen to me and you will learn of God's great wisdom and you will all benefit.*'

In Zurich, too, he had asked them '*What is the soul? What is the spirit?*' and many in the group had agreed that he must have some spiritual connection with the great Austrian philosopher Rudolf Steiner, who died in 1925 at the age of 64 – but not before he founded a new spiritual movement called Anthroposophy, which had links to European believers in trascendentalism. Steiner had spoken of the spiritual needs of people and had searched for a link between mysticism and science. Somehow, the not-so-well-read Ernani had found out about Steiner's teachings and had uttered them in his own simplistic way, so convincingly that scholars from the university had nodded their heads in agreement.

But he had taken the teachings further. Adding to Steiner's theories, he made claims of having raised the dead and, on Fridays, in a display of grand illusion, he held his hands aloft and showed his disciples the 'stigmata of Christ' – what appeared to be the scars of nails in his hands and the mark of the lance in his side. He told them that when they could not find him, it might be because he was searching for needy children in other parts of the world. He was looking after youngsters orphaned by wars in Bosnia, Afghanistan and Iraq. He had promised the children, he said, that he would return to his home in Italy and bring in money that he would then use to lift them from their misery.

Supported in his fantastic claims by Helg, Ernani came up with a new claim that left many of his followers confused and afraid: he declared that the Pope was nothing more than a figurehead and that it was he, Ernani Barretta, who was the true head of the Catholic Church.

'*Where you step, my loved ones,*' he said, casting his arm around the fast-developing grounds of his hotel, restaurant and meditation centre, '*is the heart of Christendom. It is sacred ground on which you must all tread with great respect.*'

Throughout 2002 and 2003, the complex grew. Stone pillars were erected at the entrance and a brass plate carried the name: *Rifugio Valle Grande* ('Grand Refuge in the Valley'). But Ernani liked to call it his 'paradise on earth' and as a tribute to the greater God he erected an enormous white stone figure of Jesus, 6m high, which overlooked a helicopter pad, the tarmac of which was painted with a large letter 'H' to pinpoint the landing spot. In time, disillusioned sect members were to say the real significance of Jesus and the 'H' was the son of God looking down on Hell, for that was what Ernani's headquarters had become to several of them.

They were not allowed to speak to one another without asking his permission, they claimed. While they felt obliged to hand over whatever money they had, and whatever new funds came in to them, in order to help the unfortunate that Ernani spoke of so often, they had to virtually beg for food when they were themselves hungry. Food and lodgings were free in that they did not have to pay specifically for such basic needs, but the reality was they were paying dearly by sacrificing everything they had for a cause whose results they had yet to see, except for the increasingly luxurious surroundings of Ernani's complex. Desperate to talk to someone as they did penance of sorts, many found themselves making secret phone calls to their former friends in other parts of the world, telling them of their mental torment: they wanted to be free of that place, yet Ernani's needs were so great, their beliefs in him so strong, that they felt compelled to stay.

In time his good disciples, those named after the saints, lost their roles as Ernani found a new means of keeping them under his control. He gave them belittling names, by rotation, so that there would always be a number of them who would be despised by the other members and it would be the responsibility of those so condemned to win respect so that those burdensome mantles could be passed on to others. Later sect members were to tell of the names that were given – 'bitch', 'Judas', 'unbeliever', 'madman', 'villain'. The worst was 'Black Peter', who in some mythical Christmas stories is a wicked, devilish assistant of St Nicholas. In parts of Europe he has been portrayed as a monster with a red tongue, horns and long hair. In Ernani's centre, whoever was given this name for an indiscretion would be totally outcast for however long the title clung to him.

In general, the women of the valley sect were told that they were like the mother of God, devout and pure. They could only remain that way, however, if they refused to fraternize with the opposite sex. They should even avoid looking at any male – except the Son of God himself, in the earthly form of Ernani Barretta. Sect members were to tell later how Ernani insisted that only by having sex with him, and him alone, could their bodies be cleansed of all ill, their blood made clean for the service of God. His semen was the blood of Christ.

Helg Sgarbi as he was now calling himself, at least for the time being, was as much under Ernani's influence as the others. He could not even take a drink of water without asking permission from the false Pope. And, if Ernani was not there, perhaps having transcendented to another land, his number one disciple – whoever that might be – would be the one to grant permission for even the most simple of requests. So, the faithful waited there, surrounded by valleys and forests and the distant mountain range, the Monti della Laga, waiting for God's goodness to come down upon them, in one way or another.

'*One day, you will see great miracles before your own eyes,*' Ernani told them. '*The power of God will be displayed and evil will be destroyed.*'

★ ★ ★

Throughout 2002, Helg Sgarbi continued to trawl the world's best hotels for the rich and lonely, returning occasionally to the valley with yet another bag of cash and another broken heart in his wake. But his Mercedes, with a small statue of Jesus on the dashboard and bottles of holy water in the boot, was not the only vehicle to pass in through the majestic gates of the Rifugio Valle Grande. Big black limousines with tinted windows would arrive from time to time and strangers in sunglasses, displaying the air of important men who were not to be meddled with, stepped from the rear seats. They shook hands vigorously with Ernani before retiring to a private part of the complex. They were, Ernani explained to his disciples, his business partners, working towards the glory of God and no-one dared to breathe a word that might begin with the letter 'M'.

Helg either believed his bad luck was behind him or his devotion to Ernani was such that he was prepared to take all manner of risks, for he was now in another role, with the complicit knowledge of his young wife. His change of name gave him an advantage. As far as the authorities were concerned, Helg Russak had gone to ground. At least, it seemed that way until the police snapped handcuffs on him in Bulach, a district of Zurich, in 2003. Police had decided to act, after all, on the threatening letter he had sent to Christina Weyer, but they had also added a charge of blackmail involving the wife of a director of a clinic near the German university town of Konstanz, which has a border with Switzerland. He was given a six months suspended prison sentence. Full of contrition, he left the court, knowing that deep down he would continue as before: if he was caught again, so be it.

No longer was his modus operandi centred around love and the gentle extraction of funds. He had now turned to hard blackmail – as one of the police statements to the Bulach court had revealed. During 2002, Sgarbi had targeted the clinic director's wealthy wife. It had worked like clockwork – seduce the woman, obtain a video of them together, send her the film and demand payment for his silence. The plot had all been carefully planned by Ernani and Helg together. Over strong black coffee in the cult's restaurant they had discussed how they could tighten the screws on Helg's conquests should they fail to show their generosity to him financially, after he had seduced them. The simple answer was to obtain irrefutable evidence of the sexual encounters. A tape recording wasn't enough but hard evidence of infidelity on video would be perfect.

Over the following months the two men checked out the equipment they would need. They selected a suitable video camera for 'street shots', but for more intimate bedroom scenes, more subtle equipment was available. They found a portable recording device to which a tiny 'buttonhole' camera could be attached. This was small enough to hide in a room. They also looked at tiny camera devices that could transmit images wirelessly to a computer in a nearby room. Video cameras attached to a laptop left open in a room would not, in 2002, have been good enough to record any action beyond a couple of feet and in darkened circumstances they would have been useless.

When the squeeze was applied and the clinic director's wife failed to be forthcoming with her money, the two men set to work. The 'actor' and the 'director' copied their 'porn' movie onto a disc, but before they slipped it into an envelope Sgarbi printed a comment that the woman's husband had made in public in which he had described her as the *'best woman in the world'*. Underneath that quote, Sgarbi wrote: *'Yes? Really?'* Then, with the envelope sealed and addressed to the woman, he called at the husband's clinic one evening and handed it to a night nurse. The wife was shocked and the police were informed. Sgarbi backed off, but Christina Weyer and her husband learned that the woman had been desperate enough to keep the affair secret and had fallen deeply into debt in order to pay her false lover. She was so upset at the trap that she had to seek psychiatric treatment.

The Weyers learned from the police files in Bulach a reference to the woman stated that she had been 'emotionally abused'.

By the end of 2002, then, Helg had been successful in making several million euros from at least two women, possibly a third – the Comtesse, who did not get back all the money that Helg had seduced from her; the English millionairess; and, most probably the clinic director's wife. Conceding that not all seduction attempts would be successful, Helg and Ernani did not give up and in time Sgarbi was to make money from another businessman's wife, from Bavaria in southern Germany, and also from a second executive's wife.

As Helg had once told more than one friend in Zurich, getting women to fall for him was easy. And, by now he could read the signs well. He could pick those women who were, what he was to describe to one former friend as '*walking a tightrope between loyalty to their husbands and [were] ready to fall into the net of infidelity*'.

In Monaco, Baden–Baden, Cannes or Geneva, they would sit at the pavement cafés reading a glossy magazine, hoping to strike up a casual conversation with a stranger on the lamest of excuses; they might be found in a remote spa or at a chic ski resort. Sometimes, it might be that he would catch a middle-aged blonde in a swish waterfront hotel bar as she sipped a Martini, while she pretended to be waiting for someone, making a show at looking at her watch as part of the great pretence. He might not move in right away, perhaps giving his prey a day or two, watching the same café or a place nearby, for experience told him that the particular woman he was watching would return to a location in which she felt comfortable.

He was able to differentiate the 'working women' – they had a different manner about them. They were confident and in total control of themselves. The lonely wives flirting with the unknown, uncertain whether to allow the approaches of a stranger to go beyond a simple conversation or whether they should in a fit of guilt and panic grab their handbag and flee home to their husbands, were equally easy for Helg's skilful eyes to pick up.

How he played it depended on his target. Age was no barrier to him, although he drew the line at any women in their 20s, no matter how wealthy they might seem, for he could be sure she had rich and careful parents who would be just a little older than him and would be sure to check him out. No, it was always better if he could pick a woman who was around his age or even older. Often, it was a case of the older the better. They were flattered more easily, believing they still had the beauty to pull a younger man.

He and Ernani had worked out a series of approaches that he should use. Apart from the obvious number one tactic – an admiring glance, a half smile at that woman sipping cappuccino at the table next to him – he should carefully study what they were reading (*'Ah, my sister reads that magazine, too!'*), whether they put sugar in their coffee (*'You can always pick someone who doesn't take sugar ...' 'Oh, why is that?' ... 'They're slimmer, have fresher skin – all of that'*). If they were smokers, immediately produce a lighter – a sure conversation starter (*'And would you like another coffee? I'm having one.'*).

And, there was a dress code. Study what they're wearing. Don't wear a suit in the café. Don't wear an open-neck shirt in the bar. Play the innocent, the little boy once-lost, but who was now making good. Talk of international connections, suggest a life of great adventure that he was enjoying, too secret to talk about in detail. Get them to chat about themselves, their husbands. If there was a hint of big money there, it would be on to the next step; if not, then he was out of there. Heartless, perhaps, but he wasn't in this game for love. He was in it for the money and the money was for Ernani and Ernani, in turn, would give it to God. Helg allowed for his own expenses, of course, for without a fat wallet, which his intended victims would be allowed to glance into at some point, it would be impossible to operate.

As each affair got under way, he contacted Ernani before he moved onto step two. Helg would lead his prey to a park or a spot beside the sea, place his arm around her, give her a kiss, allow her to return it – while Ernani filmed away. That footage might have been enough, but just to be sure they also used their camera-spy technique to record Helg and the victim in bed together. Then, it was onto stage three – Helg's recounting of a brilliant story, which all the lonely women fell for. Ernani is alleged to have devised the plot, hardly surprising perhaps, given those mysterious strangers who called at his centre in the Abruzzo valley. It was the Mafia child plot.

Helg told his victims a more polished version of the account he had given to the Comtesse, that while in the United States he had been involved in a car accident. A little girl had run out in front of his rental car. He had no hope of avoiding her and she was seriously injured. She would require months of surgery for her broken limbs and she would need skin grafts. It was all going to be very expensive which, Helg told each of his ladies, was not the biggest problem for him because he had covered so much of the cost by the insurance he already had. No ... the biggest problem was the girl's father. He was a Mafia Don. He wanted compensation for his little girl's terrible injuries. Personal compensation. It was going to run into many thousands of dollars and Helg was worried that he would not be able to pay it. The fact that he was now back in Europe made no difference to the demands because ... He would leave the sentence dangling and often it was the woman herself who completed it.

'... *Because the Mafia are everywhere*.'

Then, there would come a discussion about how he was going to manage, when the money was needed and – just what he wanted to hear, the question, the offer – could she possibly help in some way? He would shake his head slowly. He didn't want to involve her in his problems, but ...

She would insist. They would make love again. Then, he would gently mention the sum he was required to pay. A big sum. He had tried to borrow it but had been unsuccessful. Whoever could help him would be repaid, of course, and, in addition, they would be saving his life. Any woman now infatuated with her lover would find that gentle plea for help irresistible.

None of them gave a thought to the fact that they were paying off a gigolo. They had no idea he had done this before, or that he would do it again. They had no idea, either, that after the first 'instalment', there would be another request and if they backed down that there would be a further demand. If that didn't work, they would be sent a disc showing them having sex with Helg, with a warning that the next package would find its way to their husbands.

For those women who truly believed that Helg Sgarbi had opened the door to a new kind of freedom, for months, perhaps years, to come – although in most cases there was no intention to leave the husband – the shocking images were devastating. Inevitably, their first thoughts were to go to the police, then reality kicked in. That would mean their husbands would find out. They would *have* to pay up … hundreds of thousands of dollars and, in many cases, they would not be able to draw it out of their own bank accounts for fear of their husbands discovering and questioning the withdrawals. Therefore a loan was the only option and the hope that the now menacing Helg Sgarbi would go away. But, in many cases, he kept coming back.

Sometimes the method was different, a toning down of the demand for money, but it was a demand all the same. He told a 64-year-old woman that he desperately needed 1.5 million euros because a video he had made of them having sex had been stolen. He had made it, he claimed, so he could satisfy himself when she was not with him. The video was on his computer, which had been stolen and had fallen into the hands of the Mafia. The Mafia had come into play once again – the horrified victim headed for her bank.

Ernani was overjoyed. Like a scene from the old English nursery rhyme, 'the king was in his counting house, counting out his money' – or rather, the pseudo-Prince of Pescosansonesco drooling over his bundles of cash – he spent hours in his quarters, his fingers flicking through the bills. He bought land all around and put up houses on it. His empire was expanding beyond his wildest dreams.

Things were so good that the two men agreed that they did not want to kill their good fortune. They should not become too greedy. Perhaps Helg Sgarbi should be given a rest and Helg Russak should reappear … make his comeback as a respectable businessman for a while. He could even earn a proper wage. Just in case the police received word of a lot of very wealthy European women losing such very large sums of money to a smooth trickster.

PART THREE
The Road to
Susanne

SUSANNE GLIMPSES
THE GIGOLO

The small Swiss historic town of Uznach (population 5,500) lies near the eastern shores of Lake Zurich. A quiet place where not much happens, Uznach's main claim to fame, apart from the nearby St Otmarsberg Monastery, is the Kaltbrunner reed beds in the surrounding plains. Regarded as among the world's most important wetlands, the marshes are home to a large number of rare flora and fauna. More than 150 bird species can be found in the reed plains, attracting international tourists who enjoy long walks. You'll see a stork in a nest on the roof of the Storch Guest House on the fringes of the lake – but look again and you'll realize that the bird is not actually real ...

Despite this, Uznach is a seemingly gloomy place, despite the friendliness of its inhabitants and for all the attempts by travel specialists to make the town attractive to visitors. Uznach gives the impression that the world has moved on and left it behind. There's not much really to do but watch the traffic wind up and down the hilly main street or stare at the half-a-dozen sheep grazing in a small field directly across the road from the main post office. There are a few places to eat, it's true, one of the best being the Blume restaurant in the centre of town, half-way up the hill. Others include *Café Huter,* which is proud of its goulash; *Café Obertor,* which specializes in pancakes and a pizzeria and a doner kebab place.

So ... the question is, what on earth was Helg Sgarbi, a man who had dined in some of the finest restaurants in Europe with some of the world's wealthiest women, and who had lived in the very best hotels, doing now spending month after month without a break in this extremely unlikely place? The answer, of course, was that he was lying low, letting the heat die down before embarking on his next

SUSANNE GLIMPSES THE GIGOLO

'job'. And, if one thought about it, there was simply no better hideaway than a dim room overlooking a main road in a town that led to somewhere else.

★ ★ ★

In the narrow streets in the town's centre, the blue-painted *Café Obertor*, with its circular sign protruding over the street and row of window boxes outside the first-floor windows, provides simple but wholesome meals, although it's true that business has slackened off in recent years. The white plastic chairs and tables in the small courtyard beside the building, remain unoccupied for much of the day.

On the second floor, underneath two loft apartments nestling under the tiled roof and with a view out over Stadtchen Street, lived a tall, slim man, known to be an interpreter by profession. The bed-sit, which he occupied, was simply furnished; Martini posters, curiously mixed with religious pictures, on the wall were the only attempt at decoration. The occupant had held the tenancy in these somewhat bleak surroundings for several years, but he was rarely seen there.

The man's elderly landlords, Alfred and Elisabeth Holzer, had no idea that the tenant who they knew as 'Helg Russak' was, in fact, a highly skilled gigolo, who had already successfully swindled some of the wealthiest women of Europe out of millions of euros. As far as Alfred and Elisabeth were concerned, Herr Russak's long absences from town were connected to his job as a translator, especially as his business card told of his expertise in English, German, Spanish, Italian, French and Portuguese.

There was some other kind of work that he did, they believed, something linked to the Swiss government, but he had told them that he couldn't talk about it because it was secret. They were very impressed about that but agreed that it was up to him if he ever wanted to talk about that side of his business. It wasn't for them to ask those kinds of questions.

When he was in residence, Helg lived a simple, rather quiet life. He paid 500 Swiss francs a month and the Holzers wondered how he was able to afford it when his business around town seemed slack, to say the least. Who would want a translator in a place like Uznach, where almost everybody spoke German. But that was not their concern. Herr Russak paid his rent and he kept his room in immaculate order, so much so that they likened it to the barracks of a soldier under the eye of a fierce sergeant major. But yes, they agreed that he seemed to be struggling on the job front and they were not surprised to learn that he had put up fliers around town and also advertised his interpreting skills in local publications. Even so, there was no sign that his business was flourishing.

When the Holzers told Helg that they needed to increase the rent, times being what they were, he put up his hands – hands that had held millions of euros – in feigned horror. He pleaded with them to give him more time. His business would pick up, he said, if they would just trust him. They were concerned about his lack of income when he informed them that financial concerns had resulted in him giving up the rental of a garage where he housed his Mercedes S 300. But, it would all work out, he promised them.

Helg's biggest concern was to remain as anonymous as he possibly could – he couldn't be seen to be locking himself away, therefore raising too many questions about his life; alternatively, by making his presence felt too strongly in the town, he would attract too much attention. So, true to the form of a man determined to give the impression of someone living an unspectacular life, he strolled through the main street from time to time, eating occasionally in the *Café Obertor* restaurant and sometimes in the nearby *Café Huter*. He worked hard at being 'ordinary', but occasionally he slipped up – as with his business card when he ordered cards from a local printer on the first occasion, he asked for the name *Russak* to be embossed on them, but the second time he ordered cards bearing the name *Sgarbi*. Even so, shop owners around the small town agreed that '*Russak/Sgarbi*' – whoever he was – came across as personable and was not one to draw unnecessary attention to himself.

Now and then he would catch the eye of a woman whom had given him a second glance, more out of curiosity than anything else, and because he was also single, reasonably good looking, without being exceptionally so, and lived alone in a rented room. He would return the smile automatically. Old – and present – habits, die hard, after all.

When he called in at the local bank from time to time to cash a small cheque for work he had picked up through his simple translation business, several young female tellers would blush. He could imagine them thinking, '*Look, he's here, that nice quiet man who lives up the street!*'

People who lived near him thought he was sober and polite. No-one could have guessed his true circumstances and his connections to Ernani Barretta, with his luxurious villa in Italy.

Somehow, like a man doing penance, Helg put up with life in Uznach. The fact that he was able to reside there for months on end and put up with such miserable surroundings was testimony to his willpower – and certainly also to his devotion to Ernani Barretta.

If Helg had put aside just 10 percent of the money he had made from his exploits, he would be wealthy enough to live it up in a very fine apartment anywhere in Europe. But that would have drawn attention to him. And, after his narrow escape from jail following his dealings with the Comtesse, it was essential that he kept a low profile.

When he looked out of his bedsit window did his conscience prick him, at all? Directly across the street from him was an old Catholic church, bearing a huge stone carving of St Michael spearing Satan with a lance; beside it was a carved caption declaring that the saint protected the righteous in the fight against evil. Perhaps the significance of this never quite struck him – that perhaps one day, if he continued his life in the way that he had been up until then, he, too, could eventually face justice and he might not be so fortunate that next time.

∽

She grimaces over her cup of double espresso coffee at the coincidence when she learns that the Comtesse who was so cruelly treated by Helg Sgarbi was also called Verena. But the Verena of Uznach is less than half the age of the elderly woman. She is a successful businesswoman, a designer, who enjoys reading the morning papers at Café Huter, a comfortable little place with floral lampshades and black-and-white photos of old Uznach on the wall.

A dark-haired woman with warmth in her eyes and a certain softness to her voice, she has one thing in common with the Comtesse – she, too, was approached by Helg. But she saw in him what others before her had seen far too late … a flash of temper that left her feeling uneasy. She feels grateful that her intuition warned her to have no further dealings with him.

'He phoned me one day out of the blue offering his services as an interpreter,' she explains. 'As it happened I was looking for someone to translate documents from German into English, so I arranged to meet him. I'd seen him in the street from time to time, always casually dressed, but had never spoken to him. I knew where he lived, in that room in the Obertor – everybody knew that – but I knew absolutely nothing [else] about him. He was business-like and courteous on the phone and I saw no reason to reject his approach.

'When we finally met to discuss a possible business arrangement he began telling me all kinds of stories about himself that I just found difficulty in believing. He gave me the impression that he'd travelled everywhere doing the most important jobs and had even worked as an interpreter at the World Economic Forum.'

That claim may have had some truth to it, for his parents had a villa in Davos, where the international forum is held. In order to impress Verena further, he told her that he had worked as a translator for some social welfare groups – a touch of the good Samaritan, he might have thought, wouldn't go amiss here.

'There was something about him that just didn't seem right to me,' she continues. 'He was pushing too hard about all the worthy things he had done; it was all a bit over the top and he made me feel uneasy. It's one thing to give someone your business background but this was just too

much information and I was getting a little anxious about continuing a conversation that might lead to a business arrangement I was not happy with – mainly because of his personality more than anything else.

'Ultimately, we got around to talking about his particular translating skills and it was almost a relief to realize that I wouldn't be able to do business with him after all. My clients needed absolute exact translations from German into English and he couldn't offer that – he could only do an approximate translation, giving the sense of a document. There was no doubt in my mind that he was anxious to get work from me but I told him I couldn't help him. It was then that he just changed.

'On realizing I wasn't interested in proceeding, the warmth – what there was – suddenly drained from his face and I could see the anger there. He stared right into my eyes and I felt very disquieted, to be honest. I'd picked something up in his manner before that change so perhaps a guardian angel was looking down on me.

'Some time later he just disappeared from town and I didn't see him again until, of course, it was all in the papers. When I saw his picture I was shocked, having come so close to this man, although I must say that he did not lay on the charm in a way that he might have thought I would fall for him. I think he realized that I wasn't one of the wealthy women that he was looking out for. No, with me, it was strictly business and I'm just so glad that alarm bells rang and I was able to turn him down.'

∽

At the newspaper kiosk by the railway station a woman in her 30s leaving the train from Zurich recalls a conversation with Helg when he asked her about the dog she was walking.

'He was interested in knowing what breed [my dog] was and seemed to be trying to get into a conversation with me. I knew he was the man from the Obertor – you can't help knowing who's who in a small place like this – but that's all I did know about him. Me and everybody else. It's a bit spooky now to think that there might have been an ulterior

motive in his friendliness. He would have soon found out that I'm married in any case, but it was just the way he was coming on to me. I didn't like it at the time and thought afterwards that perhaps I was being a bit unfair and perhaps he was just a lonely man looking for a female friend.

'Now I know what was going on with him it shows my intuition was right after all.'

∽

Sometimes in the late afternoon Helg could be seen strolling up the hill – it takes just five minutes to walk from the bottom of the main street to the top and three minutes to walk back down – to a road junction near a small statue of Jesus, where he paused on a small bridge to stare out across the fields to the distant mountains. His hands would grasp the metal rail and he appeared to be deep in thought. Was he dreaming? … Or scheming?

At such times, those who saw him picked up on his loneliness, but was this a deliberate pose – all part of an act by a man who wanted to convey the impression of being completely alone and unloved, without a friend to turn to? Perhaps it was a dress rehearsal for what was to come.

It is not enough to judge a person by behaviour alone, as many in Uznach, understandably so, had done. What is in the mind is more important than what is shown in action. Some, like the women who had crossed Helg's path in Uznach and even the council clerk he stalked at a much earlier stage when she had turned down his attempt to coerce her into giving him a new identity card, were in agreement that there was a deep burning anger that could suddenly flare up. So, perhaps the calm man on the bridge, gazing at the mountains, was not all he seemed to be.

What is fascinating about Helg Sgarbi's personality, however, was that each new 'conquest' never seemed to be quite enough and the contrast between Mr Nice Guy and Mr Bad Guy became increasingly more striking.

SUSANNE GLIMPSES THE GIGOLO

There are some in Uznach who believe that should they speak out about the seemingly quiet man who had the room above the *Obertor* – that he will return with vengeance in his heart. Few know the finer details of his exploits, but they have heard the whispers around the town about his unpredictable nature and that's enough for them to maintain their silence. Among this group, Helg Sgarbi has been judged – and found guilty – of inducing unease in people, bordering on fear.

★ ★ ★

Back in Pescosansonesco, Ernani was believed to be sleeping with his female disciples – including Helg's own wife, some of his former followers were to claim. He seemed to be gloating over the money that he had earned, from Helg's exploits among others, and wondering where he should invest it next.

He had always loved cars, of course – had known them inside out since he was a kid – and he had longed to own something stylish himself. Now, the time had come it seemed and the garages he had built at Rifugio Valle Grande were gradually filled with some beauties – Lamborghini, Porsche, Ferrari. He had promised himself a Rolls Royce, too.

Unable to bank the huge stash of cash that had been delivered to him by his *Numero Uno* disciple – because it would raise eyebrows, if nothing else – he was reduced to laundering it through the houses he was building and the cars he collected. He was also working on plans to send large sums overseas, but again he had to be careful, for large transactions would ring alarm bells and lead to all kinds of questions from the authorities. He would be able to legitimately carry many thousands of euros out of Italy, but, where possible, he would use others to do it. He had relatives who would love a trip to the countries in which he had contacts and where he intended to invest in building developments, among them Croatia and Egypt.

As for the rest of the money, what to do with it was a problem, it was true. He couldn't continue to buy things around the district and he couldn't endlessly send people overseas with bundles of euros stuffed in their suitcases. The simple answer, it seemed, was that he needed to create his own bank. A very unusual bank, it seemed. The vaults would be the flower pots, garden beds and rockeries, around the restaurant complex. And just to be sure that he knew where it all was, he sketched out a treasure map, using a child-like code, so that if it fell into the wrong hands – the authorities – they wouldn't be able to understand it. At least that is what he hoped. His clues included *'red wine near the big oak'*, *'the front wall under Sandra's house'* and *'about 200 litres of good wine'*, the litres were actually a reference to a possible hidden cache of two hundred thousand euros.

Ernani Barretta had never felt so secure in his whole life. His female flock was working in the restaurant and the men were keeping the grounds tidy. From time to time he reflected on what a successful businessman he was, for his restaurant was doing well, with politicians, celebrities and wealthy individuals, personalities from all over Italy, calling by. An excellent pasta cook himself, he would have done all right from the proceeds of his fine menus alone, but these days *that* was mere pocket money.

As the months ticked by, he began to think that it was time for Helg to start working for him again. He, Ernani, had only to snap his fingers and Helg would set forth on his next romantic mission. He called Helg and summoned the Swiss Casanova back to Rifugio Valle Grande for a detailed discussion of how to proceed. In any case, he told the man, Helg's wife was missing him!

After his good fortune in escaping a jail sentence following his failed attempt to extort just about everything the Comtesse Verena had, they had agreed that Helg should keep well away from the South of France, where his face was too well known – and that may have explained why on some occasions he had failed to land a wealthy widow in that region.

Certainly, older women seemed to be much more on their guard after the events involving the Comtesse and her 'fiancé', something that was still talked about more than three years later. In any case, there were plenty of rich women frequenting the luxury spas of Switzerland, Germany and Austria and it would be easy for Helg to switch back to being simple 'Herr Russak' and take up residence in his modest apartment in that dreadful town, whatever the results of his next series of missions might be.

If, on the other hand, the authorities were trying to keep track of Helg, they would have noted that, on the face of it, he now had settled into good employment with Switzerland's second largest mobile phone company. This was in between his more leisurely work as an interpreter.

★   ★   ★

Helg's colleagues at the phone suppliers agreed that he was a complex character but in his role of dealing with dissatisfied customers he was the best. He could read people well and knew exactly how to address them. One former colleague felt that within a few seconds he could size someone up and recognize their weaknesses. Yet, in a flash he could turn from being a pleasant work colleague to a fearless creature who found it easy to tell one employee that the Mafia would enjoy tying a weight around his feet and tossing him into a lake.

He also talked of religion, of his love for Jesus. Disbelievers, he said, would wade through rivers of blood until they recognized the name of the Lord Jesus. The Nazis, the Stalinists, those who failed to recognize the gift that God had given in the form of his son would perish in hell. Religious artefacts, they saw, lay around his car or dangled from the rear-view mirror. Along with the several bottles of holy water that he carried in his boot was a well-thumbed prayer book.

But he said strange things at times. He told his colleagues of the grand adventures that he had had as a special investigator for the government, but they could never be sure what he was actually referring to. He suggested to one workmate that he was meeting his wife for dinner later, yet he had claimed to another that his wife had left him after the trauma of a second stillbirth. Curiously, although he was doing so well for himself, he tried – as he had years before with a college friend – to persuade another man at the phone company to travel to the ski resort of St Moritz and flirt with rich women who would pay for sex. In fact, he added, he knew of an experienced gigolo who could help with the 'training'. The discussion went no further than that and the colleague had no idea that the gigolo Helg was referring to was actually himself.

He also told a younger colleague, to whom he had played a father figure, that there might come a time when bad things would be heard about him. '*You will hate me and you will curse me,*' Helg told the younger man. '*All of you will condemn me.*'

When the employee later told his colleagues about this, some of them likened the comment to Jesus at the last supper.

Much later, after Helg had moved on from the company, he claimed (probably untruthfully) that he had had a secret affair with a woman who worked there. When it ended she was so emotionally hurt that she could not face the real world any more and went off to live in a convent.

His colleagues concurred that Helg Sgarbi – as he was known to them – was a self-indulgent fantasist. A religious fanatic. And, very dangerous. Particularly to women.

★ ★ ★

The next casualty of his charm was the wife of a high-powered businessman, a woman who, by reading up all he could about her and her family and by casual questioning, Helg found out was unhappy and looking for something to lift her out of the drudgery of daily life. The perfect catch.

But Helg could not ensnare this lady in on his own. With each secret rendezvous with the targeted woman that I shall call 'F' the God-like hand of Ernani Barretta had a finger on the buttons of a video recorder.

When Ernani drove back to his estate in the mountains he was accompanied by a large bag of money which the lady had handed over. Helg's latest conquest had paid off well. It was either pay-up or say goodbye to her marriage.

SUSANNE GLIMPSES THE GIGOLO

★ ★ ★

Following the months of his self-imposed exile in the apartment over the *Café Obertor*, Helg was now back on a roll. As he had told his former college friend years earlier, it was easy to extract money from the rich and lonely – you just had to know how to pick them.

One of his greatest conquests so far, he and Barretta were to agree later, was the 67-year-old wife of a furniture millionaire, who had four large stores located around Bavaria. Helg had done his homework on the woman, who I shall call 'H', and discovered that her favourite haunt was the Grand Hotel Spa Resort.

An award-winning luxury 'wellness' retreat, the hotel is located in the small Swiss town of Bad Ragaz, lying in the St Gallen Rhine Valley at the foot of the Pizol. Since the 1200s, pilgrims have made the journey through the mountains to bathe in the thermal waters that bubbled up from the earth – later confirmed to have great healing powers by the 16th century philosopher, Paracelsus. They still believe it today, those wealthy visitors who take each step towards the waters with reverence.

The hotel, with its separate apartment complexes and massive lawns, dominates the town and the mountain overshadows the hotel. The liveried doorman at the foyer entrance stares at each arrival – no-one who isn't dressed for the part dares to venture past him. A penthouse suite costs 7,500 euros a night and every inch of space, as might be expected, was filled with grandeur. In such settings in 2005, the wealthy were not on their guard. Far from home, with only their own self-indulgences to concern them, they were vulnerable. So for Helg it was easy to start a conversation with 'H'.

༄

'They walked around the town like a couple who had known each other for years,' says a shop owner who remembers the man who introduced himself as Helg – a name unusual enough for him to recall the couple.

'They seemed very much at ease with one another and at first I thought this was mother and son but when I saw his hand gently touch hers I realized there was more to it than this. You can remember them because they made such an unusual couple, once you realized they were not mother and son. Girlfriend and boyfriend ...? It was just crazy.'

The 'spa village', as Bad Ragaz proudly announces itself, is a chic community where you can almost smell the wealth, for the perfumes are the best and the clothes that the guests of the Grand Hotel wear are designer outfits. They arrive with Louis Vuitton luggage, dress in Burberry for the winter and Prada for the summer and while away the hours gazing in the windows of boutiques, art galleries and jewellers, perhaps purchasing a valuable souvenir to take home.

The pavement cafés are crowded in the summer, champagne glasses glinting in the sun. Among the laughing visitors were Helg and 'H' who are believed to have been the couple who sat for a time at the Café Huber in the town centre watching the world amble by.

They still come in their droves today, the wealthy visitors from all around Europe, and the surroundings have lost none of their charm. Elderly women, travelling in twos and perhaps widowed and rich – perfect targets for a new 'Helg' should another like him saunter into town – sip herbal tea and pick at small fruit-filled pastries, their make-up heavy in an attempt to regain the years that have gone for ever. The tourists carry the latest, tiny, digital cameras and point them at the mountains, the river and the bronze statues that stand in the street.

∽

Had Helg Sgarbi been able to pause beside one of the creations he might have chuckled inwardly at the depiction of the 'haves and have-nots', for two of the figures depict a man with a pheasant turning his back on a pleading, poverty-stricken human. Helg might have thought as he clutched his elderly girlfriend's hand that there were easier ways than begging. You just had to know how to play the game and where to go to play it. Health and wealth ... find where the two come together and there will be someone there seeking something more in their lives than the world they had left behind for a few weeks. And, calling on his past experiences, it had become clear to him that 'H' was lonely. Lonely in her marriage. Alone, wallowing in her wealth.

Even today, when his photo is shown to business people, there is a flash of recognition. He is remembered because of his elderly companion ... Such an odd couple is the general response. Definitely not mother and son, they say, unless, of course there was something strange in the relationship ...

'He would put his arm around her and I remember how he once kissed her on the cheek,' says a businesswoman. 'You couldn't help but notice and you had to wonder what he was up to. It was him working on her, you could see that, rather than the other way around.

'You could tell by her manner and her clothing that she had money. She was one of those women who went to great lengths to make herself look nice. She obviously spent a lot of time at the hairdresser's, with her hair highlighted and her general appearance being what I would describe as immaculate – as good as she could possibly make herself, given her advancing years. What I've learned about him really saddens me. You have to feel so sorry for the woman – she gave the impression of really liking him.'

They walked together through a thermal ravine to the waters where ancient kings and princesses once bathed. Helg and his new friend bathed together, too, and enjoyed candlelit dinners, sometimes in the town and a few times in one of the hotel's restaurants. She had taken the bait and when they finally parted he sent her an email speaking of his great love for her, telling her she was an extraordinary woman who was full of life and that sometimes it takes courage to love, as she had.

She could not resist his charm. The relationship grew, they arranged to meet in hotels where they could be intimate and no-one would know about it. No-one, that is, except Ernani and his recording equipment and, of course, her husband should the disc ever fall into his hands.

Then, during pillow talk on one occasion, a mask of worry hiding his face, Helg hesitatingly told her, with all the practiced skill of a brilliant actor, of the death threat that was hanging over him because he had badly injured the child of a Mafia Don in a car accident in America. He told 'H' that he faced two problems – either being severely injured or even killed by Mafia henchmen, or, what he equally feared, was the Mafia Don insisting the police take action against him. He would end up in jail and there it would be 'arranged' for him to be raped.

'H' fell for his lies, giving him 600,000 euros on his promise that it would be repaid. He had a business trip to make to Rome, but he would be back, he assured her – but 'Rome' turned out to be Pescosansonesco on the opposite coast of Italy, where Ernani distributed the cash among his various 'vaults'. His story of his laptop, carrying intimate images of the two of them, being stolen by the very same organization that had its hooks into him, terrified 'H'. It would be the end of her marriage if her husband got to hear of this but Helg had one more twist of the screw remaining. He told her that he had been warned that unless he handed over a further 1.5 million euros the images would be posted on the internet – and the problem was, her face was easily recognizable. She paid up again, handing him the money, packed into a plastic bag, at the Grand Hotel Resort, where the affair had begun.

Distancing himself as the actual blackmailer, he had yet another proposal to put to the businessman's wife: as he was so much in love with her – and he knew 'H' was in love with him – he suggested that she leave her husband and then they could buy a villa on Lake Zurich, where they could sit peacefully on the veranda and enjoy their new lives together. She was not to know that while he was seeking to control her and any other funds she possessed in her marriage, Helg himself was under the control of Ernani Barretta. But she hesitated. She asked for time. She went home, wondering if she should consult a lawyer …

★ ★ ★

SUSANNE GLIMPSES THE GIGOLO

Helg had by now realized that thermal spas offered the best selection of victims for him. After the many thousands of miles he had covered in his hunt for gullible and vulnerable women he weighed up the advantages and disadvantages of hotels, cafés, bars and health resorts. In many cases, the single women who loitered around hotels were high-class prostitutes. Those who sat in cafés with a magazine, showing long and beautiful legs that matched those of the models on the glossy pages, were on the edge of trying something new but were not sure about taking the risk. And the attractive women he found in bars often turned out to be businesswomen on a quick visit to town and were due to check out in a day or so.

But the health spas were a different matter altogether. While couples did check in, the more exclusive locations tended to attract single, wealthy women whose domestic chores, loneliness, tiredness, a general feeling of being run down, resulted in them leaving their city lives behind to breathe in the fresh mountain air.

Helg opened his laptop computer and began searching out the best resorts – but this did not preclude him from keeping his eyes open in every city he visited. He chatted to strangers, mostly women, sizing them up, for there was never any intention of forming a normal friendship with anybody. He made it known that he was an expert in finances and, with his experience from Suisse Bank behind him, he was able to convincingly 'talk the talk'.

His name got around in places where his face and his reputation were not known. A 50-year-old executive chairman of a company that manufactured parts and accessories for motor vehicles and their engines, who I shall call 'G', was introduced to the innocent-faced Helg after being urged to contact him about financial matters. A friend had told her that he personally knew Josef Ackermann, the high-powered chief executive of Deutsche Bank in Switzerland. Anyone who knew Ackermann was worth knowing, she thought. When they eventually met in an Innsbruck hotel she was overwhelmed by his youth-like aura and she was captivated when he spoke of his younger days as an unwanted child who had had to look out for himself since he was 17 years old.

She fell for him, head over heels and an affair soon began between them. She was so infatuated with Helg and the stories he, as a former military officer, told her of dangerous assignments abroad on behalf of the government that she even took the risk of telling her youngest child about him, describing him as 'James Bond'.

Thus, 007, alias Helg Russak-Sgarbi, had materialized once again, just as he had appeared before Comtesse Verena. Convinced that her lover was a man of the world, it was easy enough for him to repeat the Mafia-child lie – and 'G', just as others had done before her, began to hand over her cash.

They travelled around Europe together, snatching intimate weekends in hotel rooms. How it would end, he could not predict, but he would keep 'G' until she decided enough giving – financially that was – was enough.

In June 2007 the ritzy winter sport resort of Kitzbühel – 'Kitz' to locals – was bustling with tourists who had arrived to enjoy the mountain walks and other summer activities. They ambled through the warm streets of the mediaeval walled town, taking photos of the churches and other historic buildings, perusing the tourist shops and chatting over coffees in the pavement cafés. Among the crowds were a slim man and his older female companion.

Helg Sgarbi and 'G' were enjoying that Saturday 23 June 2007, her arm linked in his, a friendly kiss between them now and then portraying the intimacy they shared. They looked like lovers on their first weekend away together.

It was just a glance, but another visitor, a woman with short blonde hair, looked twice at the couple, believing that she recognized the love-smitten female tourist despite the sunglasses she was wearing. But yes, of course – it was 'G', an acquaintance, whose sons went to the same school as her own boys.

The woman who watched the couple thought that 'G' appeared to be very much in love with the stranger who accompanied her, but that was none of her business. She was here with her husband, in the same resort in which they had been married years before, but this time it was to enjoy the birthday festivities of a friend. As she was soon to find out, 'G' was there for the same reason – but by the time 'G' was stepping onto the cable car to go up the mountain to join in the celebrations, her male companion had slipped away. It seemed that 'G' was anxious to ensure that, among people she knew, her companion should remain a secret.

It was a just a passing moment, that scene of the couple stealing a kiss as they strolled through the crowds, and had it not been for the extraordinary events that were to follow, the woman who witnessed those few passionate seconds might have forgotten all about it. For the time being she did.

Susanne Klatten turned her thoughts back to the birthday party. With her husband Jan, she headed towards the cable car.

WICKED PLANS

Her own dark glasses gave her anonymity. They provided protection from the glare and protection from recognition – not that many people knew who she was even if she should step outdoors without making an effort to hide her identity. That was her reward for keeping a low public profile for most of her adult life. But there were times when she just wanted to mingle with the crowd, just like everyone else, just as she did that weekend, although there was always a bodyguard discreetly following behind. Even when she was with her husband, Susanne Klatten, a woman with such enormous wealth – billions of euros – could take no chances.

Was it a mere coincidence that Helg Sgarbi was in Kitzbühel that weekend when one of the richest women in the world was visiting? It was, quite possibly, mere chance, for Susanne and 'G', his companion at the time, shared the friend in common, who was having the birthday celebrations. Susanne did not exchange greetings with 'G' as the only time she had seen her was when she had spotted her with her companion, someone she obviously didn't want people to see. But perhaps 'G' had inadvertently spoken about Susanne to Helg at an earlier stage, perhaps in answer to some casual questions thrown out by the gigolo as he wooed her? It would have been easy enough for him to strike up a conversation about BMW, for he merely needed to ask 'G' if her company supplied parts for the automobile giant. It is also possible that perfectly innocently, 'G' had noticed Susanne in the Kitzbühel crowd and had pointed out the shy, wealthy woman to him.

But there was another 'coincidence', if indeed that sighting at Kitzbühel was that. For in those lazy, hazy summer days of 2007, 'G' and Helg checked into the Lanserhof Spa where, in weeks to come, Helg was to return alone and sew the seeds of what was to be his greatest and most daring caper, one that was to shock European society when the extent of it became known. Not that he didn't know the luxurious healing centre well – he had trawled it on several occasions in the past in his quest for victims.

Only Helg Sgarbi knows the preparations that he had to make before moving in on the attractive BMW heiress – and, perhaps, of all the men of his type in Europe he was the only one who could pull it off. He knew how to wrap women around his little finger. He had the charm, the looks, the confidence and he possessed all the words calculated to send a thrill through the heart, mind and body of all his conquests, no matter their age.

'*My darling,*' he wrote to one of the women who had fallen for him and who had seized every chance to make love to him, '*never forget the passion we share. We will love one another for ever.*'

Sexual illusion. Flattery. A combination of the two, worked every time. There was the email that he had sent to 'H': '*You are a special lady to me, for you live for love and you are right to do so, because that is what life is all about.*'

He wrote to another about the liaison that they had shared on a beach and how she had '*groaned in passion*'. Helg had the words – and they were words that could be used as either an inducement for an affair to continue; or as a threat should his seduction begin to fail.

Helg had a number of other aces to play when he decided it was time to turn sex into demand: his sob stories. The Mafia was always a key player in his tales of woe; the threat to his life the main plot; the ending a need to find hundreds of thousands of dollars or it could mean unimaginable punishment.

Perhaps for his latest round of treachery he searched the internet for the wealthiest women in Europe – the very wealthiest of them all, in fact – and set himself a challenge, an audacious task: to start an affair with her.

Did he use 'G' not just as a source of sex and money, but as a means to an end – to find out whatever he could about Susanne Klatten? Mothers whose children attend the same schools tend to talk to one another – not just about their children but about themselves and each other. It would have been no trouble for the cunning Helg to establish which school Susanne's children attended and another few days of observation would have allowed him to pinpoint mothers calling to pick their children up, although in Susanne's case she did not do this herself due to the security risk.

Did Helg spy 'G' among the mothers, observe her children talking to Susanne's boys, perhaps? And did that scene provide him with his next target? In any case, his plan to move in on 'G' worked and within a short time she was telling her friends about the clever financier who she had met, a man who knew Josef Ackermann, the boss of Deutsche Bank, no less.

In the relationship with 'G' there were already too many coincidences to dismiss the notion that he had targeted her as a means to an end. And, if he could end the relationship with a large bag of money, it would be so much the better. 'G' was to tell police later that she happened to be reading a book about the Mafia when Helg revealed the 'little problem' that was troubling him. He recounted how he had been involved in an accident with the young daughter of a Mafia Don; after that, she did not need to use her imagination as to the fate that awaited her charming lover if he did not pay the Don off. Was it another coincidence that 'G' was reading about the frightening organization just at that time? Or had he perhaps suggested earlier that she read the book? Perhaps even given her a copy? Over the years Helg had certainly learned the value of preparation. Know your subject. Know *everything* about her and use pieces of that homework as appropriate.

Helg told 'G' that he had to disappear for a while. It might be for several months. He would hand the money that she had loaned him to the Mafia contact and then he would be back, he promised. She put her faith in him. And Helg Sgarbi drove out of her life, the nose of his Mercedes heading South, towards Italy, with a bag stuffed with 300,000 euros.

Months before the devastating TV documentary about the Quandts' links to the Nazi era – distant though they might be – was shown on German television at the end of September 2007, Helg began trawling for information about Susanne. There was little about her background on the internet, such was the secrecy she had placed around her life, but the gigolo was an expert at extracting information from friends of friends. What he had going for him were the wide interests he had built up over the years – banking, the military and, of course, religion among others. With all manner of people, he had discussed the spiritual world and its relation to science, picking on the ideas of Rudolf Steiner. He was well-versed in the latest technology and could converse easily on political matters. What he didn't know, he was skilful at bluffing his way through. He was a veritable master of his wicked trade.

While 'G' might have unwittingly provided Helg with a few tit-bits about Susanne, he found a source whose information turned out to be invaluable. At some stage Helg became engaged in conversation in Munich with a professor, a few years old than himself. A very special man, it transpired, for he knew everything about Susanne's search for a more spiritual life. He knew her thoughts, her holiday haunts ... the very information that a man like Helg would have happily paid dearly for. Susanne was to tell police in time that the professor was the only person outside of her family who knew such specific details about her thoughts and her travels.

How Helg gleaned the information from the professor is known only to him and the professor himself, but later Susanne had few doubts that it was the scholar who had provided the fraudster with detailed and essential information about her private life.

It is possible the man was a former friend of Helg's from his university days, or he might have been among those members of Ernani Barretta's sect who were awe-struck by the false Messiah's words. Ernani had certainly spoken of spiritual matters and how he could transfigure his body into another form, a claim that was of enormous interest to those who believed there was much more to human life on earth, but that's all conjecture.

In any case, Helg learned such details that in her search to find spirituality, Susanne had made the religious journey to the ancient St Catherine's Monastery, located at the entrance to a gorge at the foot of Egypt's Mount Sinai, where Moses is described in the Bible as having received the Ten Commandments. Susanne spent many hours in meditation there, listening to her guides tell how the Christian martyr, Catherine of Alexandria, was sentenced to death on a wheel – where the condemned were beaten through the spokes – but when that failed to kill her she was finally beheaded. Susanne also learned about one of the important events linked to the Monastery, the festival of transfiguration, the moment when a human is transformed into a divine being such as an angel.

If such a divine topic were not music to the ears of a man who believed that reaching a woman through her mind was as important as touching her body, Helg garnered more information from his learned source about Susanne's search for spiritual enlightenment. She had travelled to Jordan, to the ruins of the ancient city of Petra, which has both religious and archaeological significance.

Petra is located at the start of the Valley of Moses, the site where the Old Testament prophet is said to have struck the ground and water gushed from it. The area has great spiritual significance and its peaceful surrounds would have been therapeutic for a woman under daily pressure as one of the Queens of industrial Germany. Curiously, there were hidden meanings all around her, which would have had importance had she been able to see into the future. For some religious scholars believe that Petra is the desert place that is being prepared by God for the Jewish people and they quote a Biblical text, from Revelations, that tells how:

'The woman was given the two wings of a great eagle, so that she might fly to the place prepared for her in the desert, where she would be taken care of for a time, times and half a time, out of the serpent's reach.'

But for now, the serpent was about to start circling Susanne.

So much of Susanne's personal life was known to her mentor that she was to tell police that she was convinced that he was the only person who could have passed such information on to Helg. There was more, however. Susanne had had discussions with the professor about her thoughts regarding the motor industry and her business, about the problems that were already being examined by car manufacturers like her own BMW company as concerns grew about diminishing world oil stocks. She spoke to the academic about renewable energy, the only 'outsider' that she had had such discussions with. They talked of a future in which power would be generated from natural elements like the Sun, tides and wind. It was another topic that Helg made a mental note of – he would read all he could about the subject. It would be his homework for a while.

But there was one more vital piece of information that came his way. Perhaps the most important of all. Whether he learned it before he went to Lanserhof with 'G' or later on is not clear, but he discovered that Susanne had been a guest at that spa from time to time. It was her escape from the city; from the duties of motherhood; from the demands of her corporate interests. It was her place to refresh mind and body. What was more, she was due to check into the spa again during that July of 2007.

Soon, Helg was ready to make his play. This was the big one. If he could land this 'fish', as he was to refer to the BMW heiress to his guru, he and Ernani would never need to search for rich, lonely and, yes – *lost* – souls again.

THE SEDUCTION BEGINS

Susanne Klatten wound through the local traffic to the north of Munich. It was a sunny day in July 2007, and she was leaving behind the demands of her job as the head of BMW in exchange for a couple of weeks of relaxation in the Austrian mountains. Her destination was a health resort; it was somewhere she knew that she could renew her energy and also perhaps revive her flagging spirit.

The words in the spa's promotional brochure could not have been more applicable to Susanne's own life: '... *it is not uncommon for even the most successful people, who are steadfastly anchored in their professional lives, to suddenly experience a drop in their performance ability and experience a crisis regarding the meaning of life.*'

In recent years Susanne had been searching for a deeper meaning to life. She had talked about this only to trusted friends. And, who knew? Perhaps she might find it before her month at the spa was over.

She exited the autobahn near Innsbruck and continued heading South, changing into a lower gear to climb the winding mountain road to the village of Lans.

Tourists intending to take in the sights of Lans (population 800), just 8km (5 miles) from Innsbruck, are warned not to expect breathtaking mediaeval churches, museums, entertainment centres and the like in the centre of the village, simply because there is not much of a centre at all. But the village, with its streets so narrow that there is hardly enough room for two cars to pass each other, has been around for a long time; it was first mentioned as Lannes, on the old salt road, in 1180.

There is a quaint, comfortable, family-run hotel, the *Isserwirt*, at the roadside, with flowers cascading down from the window ledges and there are a couple of restaurants and guest houses, but the main attraction is the Lanser See, also known as Lake Lans. And the health centre, of course.

THE SEDUCTION BEGINS

From the outside, looking up towards it, the Lanserhof holistic health resort looks like a large wooden cabin with wide windows and a flat roof, tucked into the hillside. The centre boasts of taking its wealthy guests away from the drudgery of everyday life to a *'peaceful place for the senses'*; providing a *'symbiosis between Nature and architecture'*, where anyone suffering from stress can relax and rebuild. Guests determined to heal mind and body stroll about the high-tech areas in white bathrobes, nodding greetings to one another, but a visit there is not about making conversation. It is to lose oneself in tranquility. A two-week minimum stay is required in order to achieve what the medical staff say will be meaningful and long-term regeneration and for the treatment alone – a general medical examination, massages, daily therapy, medical lectures and fine foods – the cost runs to almost 2,000 euros, with an additional bill for the accommodation. It can take up to three months to get a room there.

Architect Dr Regina Dahmen-Ingenhoven designed a complex which, she said, *'must receive the people with open arms'*; the hotel is, therefore, very welcoming. There is soft, piped music and rooms are decorated in soft colours and with stripped-pine and soothing white furnishings. They also have log fires for winter stays. The resin walls send out a sci-fi greenish glow, while guests follow mosaic tiles to day beds, where they can be cocooned against the outside world. But the outside world at the Lanserhof is also worth looking at, for there are breathtaking views of the surrounding mountains and valleys.

Discretion is the hotel's highest priority. Andreas Wieser, the man in charge, insists that the identity of his clients remains strictly confidential, but that does not prevent word of the exclusive guest list leaking out: in 2006, for example, Roman Abramovich, the Russian oil tycoon and Chelsea Football Club owner, was a guest, accompanied by an entourage of friends, bodyguards and aides. The entire visit by the world's 20th richest man – he has a personal fortune of £10.8 billion – was said to have cost him £600,000, including the charge for rooms and treatments for his entire staff.

As part of the health treatment, Susanne, like all other guests, was asked to fill in a form, so that the medical staff could prepare a specialized recovery programme. '*Individualized care is very important to us,*' the resort tells its guests at the top of the health history form. It asks for the guest's birth date, height, profession, working hours and hobbies. Some of the questions are deeply personal, asking women about their menstrual cycle, whether they are beyond menopause, if they have had any miscarriages and what their known illnesses or allergies might be. The questions also delve into the patient's family background – has there been any alcoholism, thyroid or rheumatic illnesses among family members?

Only the management and the individual doctors involved in Susanne's treatment know if she revealed her real identity. It is likely that she did: even if she had not stayed there before, it is probable that a member of the staff would have recognized her. But whatever Susanne expected when she arrived at the Lanserhof, she could never have imagined how her stay there would unravel.

The resort, which promises '*the medicine of the future*', offers specialist treatment for insomnia, digestive problems, obesity, memory loss and '*loss of libido*'. But the man who checked in on 12 July, three days after Susanne had arrived, had no trouble with his libido, as a string of heartbroken women could well have testified.

Helg Sgarbi had arrived at the Lanserhof for one reason only. To begin the careful and calculated seduction of the BMW heiress – a plot that on the face of it seemed absolutely impossible and one that bordered on madness. How he had managed to secure a room at what is believed to be short notice is unclear. One thing is certain though, he definitely stood out among the male guests, who were themselves outnumbered by women, since almost all of the men were several years older and many spoke neither German, French nor English.

In the first few days, Helg became accustomed to a breakfast that began with toast and lunch that consisted of a few vegetables. There was always herbal tea on hand; guests could simply help themselves at any time of the day. He was not expecting to dine in grand style here, despite the fact that the hotel employed top-grade chefs to use the most modern of cooking techniques to ensure '*that the maximum on vital nutrients is retained*'. No alcohol was allowed; no caffeine and there was a no-smoking policy, one which the Russian guests tended to ignore, puffing away in the hotel grounds at every opportunity.

But Helg was not concerned with any of this – his attention was focused on the blonde woman who strolled about the spa.

Susanne Klatten had been in-house for several days now and she had more than a week to go. Perhaps she was already feeling that the pressures of her life in Munich – the combination of having to make high-level decisions on the BMW advisory board while also being a mother to her three children – were falling away. The demands of combining a professional life with motherhood had not been easy for Susanne, although she gave every appearance of coping. She and her husband, Jan, were the picture of happiness – the few photos of the couple that had been taken at official functions gave the impression of a husband and wife contented with their lot and there was absolutely no doubt that their marriage was founded on love in the days when Jan had courted BMW's 'canteen lady' without knowing her true identity.

The events that were to follow after Susanne checked into the Lanserhof perhaps suggest that her marriage might also have been under some stress, even before she met Helg Sgarbi.

Even at home, away from industrial plants and boardrooms, the signing of documents and the tough decisions that had to be made, there could be no escape from her company affairs, for Susanne and her husband were deeply involved in discussions to buy into Nordex, a major wind-turbine maker – and Jan was also involved in the day-to-day management of his wife's 9-billion-euro fortune. Business dominated Susanne's days and nights. There was little or no relief from it. Perhaps this had led her to ask herself if she was really happy and, if her answer was negative, what she could do about it. Her search for some kind of spiritual release suggested that if she found an answer, she would grab it. Protected by bodyguards for as far back as she could remember and wary of strangers as a result of her family background, at Lanserhof she perhaps felt that she could let her guard down. She had placed herself in the hands of medical professionals, but, in reality, to anyone wishing to take advantage of her – someone staying at the spa for less than altruistic reasons – she was vulnerable.

She threw on her white bathrobe and switched her mind to the relative quiet of her surroundings. There were no phones, no computer screens and certainly no sound of roaring traffic whenever she stepped outside. Her days consisted of sitting by the pool in the warm mountain sunshine, reading a book; she had massages, walked, did Pilates, went to the gym and listened to soothing music. She sipped herbal teas and juice cocktails and attended lectures on how to balance body and spirit. By 9p.m. the day at the Lanserhof was effectively over and everyone went to bed. For some the routine, at first welcome, could quickly become boring. The simplest of distractions – a brief conversation with another guest, perhaps – could give the day an unexpected lift.

★ ★ ★

He knew when to strike. Stalking Susanne for days, watching her move about the complex, speaking to virtually no-one, he knew he had to pick his moment. Nothing too clever; nothing too heavy. A smile at breakfast; another during the day. A slight nod of acknowledgement from her at his warm but friendly greeting. He gave absolutely no indication that he knew who she was. She had to be convinced that he saw her as just another guest at the spa. He couldn't afford to blow it by giving her the impression that he knew anything about her. One mistake and he would have lost the chance to win her over for ever. *Restraint.* That was the key. So, he bided his time and throughout the first week of her stay, Susanne had no idea of the shadowy figure that trailed her every move from a suitably discreet distance.

When he judged that she had had enough of doing nothing – the signs evident in the laying aside of her book from time to time; the deep sighs; her blank gaze as she looked out across the mountains – there were only three full days to go before Susanne was due to check out. So, Helg made his move. Three days gave him enough time to work on her and the period was short enough to leave her wanting to know more about him but having to leave before the chance arose.

The moment he picked was perfect. She was sitting alone, head down in a book. It was *The Alchemist* by Paulo Coelho, a novel about a young Spanish shepherd who embarks on a journey, following a dream to find treasure in the pyramids of Egypt. Helg had known what she was reading, of course, and didn't have to do any research on it at all, for Coelho had been born in Rio de Janeiro – the very city in which Helg had grown up himself. He knew the book well. It was almost a sign. Yes, everything was perfect. It was time to strike.

The truth, of sorts, was on his lips when he casually spoke to her for the first time: '*Ah, my favourite book.*'

She looked up, laying it down. '*You've read it?*'

If he had been allowed to write the script himself that probably would have been her planned response. He had got her to ask a question to which he needed to give away information about himself.

'*I spent my childhood where the author comes from – it's been essential reading. To me, the story has been like a Bible. There's a spiritual message in it. You must believe in a dream and once you believe, you should follow it and you will achieve all that you wish for.*'

The conversation continued – the man was intriguing enough for Susanne to keep the book on her lap as she looked into his boyish face. All the years of suspicion of strangers fell away as he spoke to her. After all, there could be no safer environment than this one. And there was certainly no threat from this man, casually dressed, as he was, well-spoken, clean cut and clearly interested in more than earthly matters.

Underlying his obvious enthusiasm for the book, Susanne picked up a hint of sadness emanating from the handsome man, who was now sitting by her side. He spoke a little more about his interest in spiritual matters and about the way the world was heading. How there was all this energy all around them, but scientists had yet to find a means of utilizing it properly, making it work on large sustainable scale. His words actually echoed her thoughts. He was *such* a fascinating man.

That night in the plush solitude of his own room, with its luxurious pine wood furnishings and floors of cherry wood, Helg Sgarbi was, without a doubt, ecstatic. Everything had gone to plan. The conversation had been short, admittedly, but he had made that crucial breakthrough. She had not rebuffed him. And he had noted the sparkle in her eyes as his conversation carried her away from the demands of

1. The Goebbels family with stepson Harald Quandt. Back row from left: Joseph Goebbels, Helga, Hilde, Harald Quandt. Front row from left: Hellmut, Holde, wife Magda, Heide and Hedda – presumably 1942.

2. Susanne Klatten's parents, Herbert Quandt and his wife Johanna, photographed on 20 April 1971.

3. Hanns Martin Schleyer, kidnapped by RAF in Cologne on 5 September 1977. On 14 October 1977 the Parisian evening newspaper France Soir *and the German daily newspaper* Frankfurter Rundschau *received this picture as evidence that Schleyer was still alive.*

4. The Obertor Restaurant in Uznach, Switzerland, where Helg Sgarbi rented a modest flat. The window of his room is immediately below the loft window on the right. (Photograph: Richard Shears.)

5. Helg Sgarbi – the face that stole the heart of so many women.

6. From the nearby village of Lans, in Austria, the luxurious Lanserhof health spa looks like a long log cabin with panoramic windows. (Photograph: Richard Shears.)

7. The Rosenberger restaurant, at the Vomp rest stop in Austria, where Helg Sgarbi was to collect his blackmail money from Susanne Klatten. (Photograph: Richard Shears.)

8. Ernani Barretta, surrounded by media at Pescara's court in Italy on 24 March 2009. Barretta denied accusations that he filmed sex videos in the attempted blackmail of Susanne Klatten.

9. Helg Sgarbi in the court room before his sentencing in Munich, Germany, on 9 March 2009. The court sentenced him to six years imprisonment.

10. Susanne Klatten, photographed in May 2009, after the blackmail scandal that threatened to ruin her reputation.

11. One of the few images of the notoriously private Quandt family: Johanna Quandt and her son Stefan at a reception for the former Chief executive of BMW, Mr. Eberhard von Kuhnheim in Munich, on 6 July 1999.

12. The entrance to Ernani Barretta's Italian 'country house', Rifugio Valle Grande – closed for business while he awaited a court hearing related to money found hidden on the property. (Photograph: Richard Shears.)

13. Ernani Barretta relaxes by a fountain in the grounds of his country house, Rifugio Valle Grande. (Photograph: Richard Shears.)

the world into which she had been born to the one that she believed could exist. After days on end of doing little more than strolling, reading and sleeping, it was as if she had woken up from a stupor. And … she had agreed to go for a walk with him the next day.

So, on the following day, under a bright blue Tyrolean sky, they set out for the meadow behind the complex, strolling along a narrow path through the white, yellow and purple wildflowers, towards the pine forest, speaking of the benefits of Lanserhof but agreeing it was good to break with routine. The air was filled with the hum of bees and the scent of resin from the pines. He had not given her any impression that he knew who she was. He would let her make the introduction.

In the meantime, he told her more about himself, mixing truth with lies, the modus operandi of a conman. That which could be checked would be the truth; that which couldn't were the lies.

He spoke again of his days in Rio, how he had been born in Switzerland but had gone to Brazil with his parents at the age of five or six because his father had landed an important job there. He had returned to Switzerland in his mid-teens, attending schools there before completing a law degree at UZH. He had lost all contact with his parents at that time, he said. He had worked for Credit Suisse and, with a talent for languages – he could speak six – he had set up his own business as an interpreter, mainly translating legal documents. He was now involved in mergers and acquisitions and was called in when businesses were forced to close. He was planning, though, to move into new technology, particularly renewable energies. There was something else he was involved in, but the secrecy document that he had signed with the Swiss government prevented him from discussing it.

Why this conversation did not make her even remotely suspicious, even Susanne could not explain when she looked back on it much later. It was just too perfect – the book, the Rio background that he shared with Coelho, the subject of renewable energies which he professed such interest in and which she, of course, had been pursuing for at least a year … And there was so much more that should have set off alarm bells in Susanne's head, as they talked, wandering through the lush grass at the foothills of the Alps.

THE SEDUCTION BEGINS

Helg told her that he had travelled to the religious sites of Egypt and Jordan – just as Susanne had. But still there was no sudden flash of suspicion – after all, only her close family and the professor, who she trusted implicitly, knew of her pilgrimage to those areas. In any case, there was no reason to doubt this man who was so easy to converse with. He came across as an intelligent, clean-cut businessman, like so many of her own executives. As far as she knew, he had no idea of her identity. Perhaps she was applying the 'Jan-test' again – finding out whether the person who was making conversation with her was interested in her for herself alone and not for her wealth.

Helg meted out his information carefully. After all Susanne was not due to leave for another couple of days and she had agreed to go for further walks with him. There were ample places to stroll – a 10-minute walk down the steep hill to the village, and more tracks through the valley and up through the pine forests above the resort – so plenty of opportunity to make her feel comfortable with him. It was time to play some even higher stakes …

ॐ

'Yes, it is possible they came here,' comments a staff member at the Isserwirt hotel in the village. 'We have guests from the Lanserhof who come down here … It gives people a break, you see, and many of them are guests from up there who are alone. They come to get well but then they want a touch of something different, just now and again, so they come to the village looking for a change of environment.'

Susanne has long returned to Munich and Helg is now behind bars, but single women still flock to the spa, of course, for there is no place like the Lanserhof. You walk in through the glass doors and are confronted by a bar, but the only drinks immediately in sight appear to be glasses of tea, standing on the counter. In the lounge area a woman sits gazing through the panoramic window down over the valley to Innsbruck, a toy town far below and beyond it, the towering mountains. Another woman sits reading a magazine, one of many spread out on a low table in the lounge. In the dining room a third woman sits alone eating lunch.

It is not difficult to imagine someone with the mind-set of Helg Sgarbi stepping into this place, playing the innocent, but craftily summing up a victim. The woman in the dining room perhaps … he takes a table nearby, waits for a sign – perhaps a soft sigh or the eyes closing for a few seconds – and makes his move. An opening conversation … how nice it is to be away from the crowded restaurants of the cities … how so very relaxing it is here, you could almost go to sleep at the table … have you been down to the village yet? …

∽

He dropped a name here and there, including that of Josef Ackermann of Deutsche Bank and a reference to the bank's administration board. He had been in the military, of course, because it had been compulsory. Then, he told her, he could give her just a hint of his work, but she mustn't say anything to anyone else. Again, a clever ploy: he was sharing an intimacy with her, a special confidence only for her ears. He was involved in 'special duties', working in crisis areas for the government. He gave her the impression that he was a kind of secret agent, a man who had to rush to any number of countries to quell trouble. It was all hush-hush, but because he trusted her, he told her, he felt safe in speaking about his work in very general terms. He went on to suggest that he had been involved in dangerous hostage negotiations and had dealt with threats to national security.

For a woman who had spent her adult life under the watchful eye of bodyguards, on whom it had been impressed time and again that secrecy and discretion were of prime importance, she understood her companion's vagueness as he spoke of his life-threatening missions. His comments had even more impact as they walked through the peaceful valleys, for she was reminded once again that it was indeed a perilous and unpredictable world that she had left behind and to which she would soon have to return and be forced to lock herself away, if not physically, certainly mentally. The truth was – and she was to admit this publicly much later – she just wanted to be 'normal' like everyone else and to be regarded as such.

THE SEDUCTION BEGINS

In a curious way, Susanne Klatten appeared to be suffering from the same 'caged-tigress syndrome' as Princess Diana – untouchable, trapped in a world of duty and wealth, yet inwardly crying out for release. In the end, Diana, whether it was a response to Prince Charles' apparent indifference, turned away from her husband to other men. Now, Susanne, also powerful, rich and attractive, was teetering on the brink of infidelity.

It says much for the seductive powers of Helg Sgarbi that he was able to convince Susanne somehow that deceiving her husband and taking a gamble with him was something totally free of risk, an adventure that could open up a new and exciting world of which she had denied herself for so many years.

Susanne also found Helg intriguing as he had an inherent inner sadness. Occasionally on their walks, he would break the silence – particularly speaking of his upbringing, when as a child he felt that he had lacked the love of his parents – and she was deeply moved. Sticking closely to his mental script, Helg spoke of extremely personal matters – how he had fallen in love with a Swiss girl and had married her just the year before. But already the marriage was over and he was heartbroken.

Susanne was to tell police much later: *'He was charming, attentive and at the same time seemed very sad. That stirred a feeling in me that we had something in common.'* It was an admission for the official records that for all her billions of euros, her seemingly enviable position as the head of a successful international car company and an apparently flawless marriage, she was desperately unhappy.

'Are you divorced, then?' she asked him as they walked.

The question was again all that he had hoped for. She was becoming more and more interested in his personal life.

'Not yet,' he said, hinting that he would be a free man soon.

It was almost time for Susanne to check out. She had already asked herself, as she had on so many occasions before when introduced to people for the first time, *'Can I trust this person? Should I become involved in conversation or back off?'* By now though, after their long walks and their intimate chats over tea or outside, she had no remaining doubts about her new-found friend. She was prepared to meet him again.

By the time she left, Susanne had revealed her true identity to him and they had exchanged mobile numbers. She returned to Munich knowing that they would soon be back in touch with one another. He had touched something deep inside her, although she might not have been aware of anything more than the fact that she couldn't stop thinking about him. In the sadness that she had read behind his smile, he had stirred in her a longing to look after him. At the same time he had offered her a glimpse into a world far beyond the one in which she had so far lived. These were all new-found emotions, ones that she felt she could not share with her husband, especially as it would mean that she would have to reveal that these feelings had been spawned by another man – a disaster for even the most stable of relationships.

Helg Sgarbi spent the three days after Susanne's departure basking in his success. He had no doubt that he had caught the interest of not only the richest woman in Germany, but also one of the world's wealthiest.

Aside from her husband, who else had her personal mobile number? With who else had she shared her thoughts about spirituality? With who else had she chatted so easily and intimately? '*No-one!*' he might have shouted in answer to his own questions. '*No-one!*'

There was still a lot of work to be done before he could reel her in, and that would take more time. Ernani also needed to know that. There must be no pressure from the Italian but at the same time Ernani had to be prepared to do some more film work – and be ready to react, pretty much at the drop of a hat.

Susanne and Helg began exchanging text messages; the tone was friendly like a couple who had known each other for far more than just a fleeting few days. Whether Susanne had suggested a rendezvous with her new friend or whether Helg discovered independently what Susanne's movements were, August found them together again, this time on the French Riviera, where Susanne had a holiday home.

Perhaps Susanne had said to him: '*If you happen to be on the French Riviera next month, give me a call …*?'

THE SEDUCTION BEGINS

It is also possible that someone told Helg exactly where Susanne could be found – the same person who had told him about Susanne's visit to Lanserhof, perhaps? It would certainly have been too difficult a task for Helg to have followed Susanne from her Munich home to her holiday hideaway. She would have been immediately suspicious and alarmed had he suddenly turned up at her house unannounced.

There's also the question of whether Susanne travelled to the South of France alone. If her husband and children were with her, it would not have been easy for the couple to meet up, yet it was here, according to police sources, that they had their first sexual encounter. The likelihood is that she visited him at one of the many hotels on that expensive strip of the Mediterranean coast.

And so, it began.

Helg Sgarbi walked proudly along the Riviera waterfront. He had achieved the impossible, bagged the ultimate prize. He had seduced one of the most powerful women in Europe … make that the world! Tell that to anyone and they most probably would have laughed in his face. There might be other high-profile women who could be led astray but Susanne Klatten …? *Impossible!* But from that first secret, sexual, rendezvous, he had her wrapped around his little finger and the longer it went on, the better it would be for him.

He called Ernani. Police sources said the conversation went pretty much along the following lines.

'I have caught the big fish.'

'You have caught many big fish – which one is this?'

'The one we've discussed. Susanne Klatten, the boss of BMW.'

'Susanne Klatten? You have won over Susanne Klatten? Oh my God! This is big trouble for us.'

'No, it's not trouble. She won't make trouble. She's already in too deep with me. She has a husband. She has a reputation. A very important reputation.

'Oh my God!'

Yes, it was the start, Helg thought. He was not going to let this big fish swim away. The old, dearly departed Comtesse Verena, the English millionairess, the other executives' wives from whom he had skimmed millions … they were all small fry compared to his Susanne.

SEX, THE MAFIA AND A SECRET VIDEO

What was going through Susanne's mind after she returned to Munich and faced the demands of the corporate world from which she had briefly escaped? Could she really apply her mind entirely to her work, and the duties of motherhood, knowing that she had broken her personal code? There had been enough clues in her conversation with Helg for him to realize that she was looking for something new, certainly. But just how game was she really to allow the affair to continue? And, to what end?

Women – and men – who have affairs realize that eventually there has to be heartbreak for someone – their own, that of their lover or that of their existing partner or spouse. Susanne, on her return to the family home, was tormented, knowing that she had to see Helg again – the evidence of that being that she *did* see him. Should she say anything to Jan? Or should she allow her relationship with Helg roll on until the inevitable tragic end?

They called one another on their mobiles and sent text messages. She couldn't forget him and he certainly wasn't going to let her.

To make sure of that, Helg drove to Pescosansonesco and spoke long into the night with Ernani. They are thought to have drawn up a detailed plan which they both agreed could potentially reap them more money than they had ever dreamed of. It was for God, Ernani reminded Helg. The money would not be used for earthly gain. Susanne Klatten had simply too much wealth; it would be to God's glory if she could be cleansed of some of it. Helg agreed with his mentor's reasoning, but he also accepted Ernani's suggestion that this time he should take a little bit more of a cut for himself. *A new car to replace that old Merc, perhaps? Or a nice little home somewhere overlooking a lake? An overseas venture to some exotic location?* Any of these things, he would most definitely have earned.

★ ★ ★

Susanne was physically and mentally attracted to her chisel-featured, blue-eyed lover, whose thoughts appeared to mirror her own. They began meeting in hotels where her dependency on him as a lover intensified. They clutched hands at intimate dinners, when she was able to make plausible excuses for her absences from home. He sent her loving emails and text messages. She took several risks, for there was every chance that someone she knew or who recognized her would see her with a man who was obviously not her husband.

They arranged to meet in another 'discreet' hotel where no-one would expect to find her – the Holiday Inn in the Schwabing district of Munich. The only risk was that it was in the same district as her home, but then again, who would have expected to find Susanne Klatten there, meeting her lover? A four-star business-oriented hotel, the Holiday Inn lies to the North of the city centre. It has had mixed reviews from guests, one businessman describing the rooms in 2007, as being '*very dark*' with everything '*either dark brown or grey*' and the bathroom was of the same style as when he stayed there 30 years earlier.

But it was the perfect location for a couple keen to remain out of sight of the high end of the corporate world. On 21 August Susanne drove into the underground car park and stepped into the lift. It bypassed the reception area and took her straight up to the sixth floor. A few steps and she was tapping at the door of room 629. During that passionate afternoon, Susanne realized she was falling for her 'special agent'.

The following day Helg told her that he had been called away. An urgent assignment in his role as 'special adviser' for the Swiss Government. She knew – or thought she knew – what this meant. Another dangerous mission. He had to travel to the United States but he would call her when he returned.

True to his word, he contacted her on Sunday 26 August, sending her an SMS. In it he said that he needed to speak to her urgently and would call soon. The carrot was being dangled. When the call came, he told her that he must see her as soon as she could arrange it. Something had come up and he needed to talk to her about it. When she asked what it was, he told her it was far too dangerous to discuss it over the phone. They agreed to meet in a motel, the Tulip Inn, in the village of Schwaig, just a few minutes from Munich airport.

The three-star establishment was not of the exclusive style to which Susanne was usually accustomed, but as she arrived at the white-painted building she recognized that it was perfect for their rendezvous. Like the Holiday Inn, no-one would expect a woman of her calibre and wealth to be meeting anyone in a hotel offering anything less than five-star facilities. But the accommodation was comfortable enough, as she soon discovered when she went straight to the room where Helg had told her to go. It was the middle of the afternoon on that Sunday 26 August 2007, and the sunlight was forcing its way through the lace curtains as he ushered her inside and embraced her.

What happened next on a personal level, Susanne has never revealed – and neither has her playboy lover – but the time eventually came when he explained the urgency of his summons to her. Yes, of course he couldn't wait to be with her again, but something had happened, something dreadful. An incident had occurred during his trip to the United States, one which explained his hurried return. Susanne was not to know at that time that the 'United States' was really Pescosansonesco, Italy. Helg continued his well-rehearsed story, adding a few modifications for effect.

He had gone to Miami, not in his role as an agent, as he had hinted, but in his profession as a consultant in the merger-and-acquisition business. He was driving fast in his rental car on a narrow road when a little girl suddenly ran out in front of him and he didn't have time to stop. She had been seriously injured and there were fears she would never walk again. This was awful enough but he was in far more serious trouble because the child was actually the daughter of a Mafia Don. He now needed a fortune to pay off the father who was making threats against him. Helg had been extremely lucky to leave the country when he did, before he was hurt by the Mob. Now, he said, even the very best Swiss lawyer could not help him. His problem wasn't a legal one. The girl's father didn't care about going through the courts. He just wanted cash. And, as an important member of the Mafia, he had plenty of contacts in Europe to ensure that he got it.

'*What he's asking for is effectively a ransom,*' Helg said, his face the very picture of misery. '*The payment to be made is not only for compensation, but is in exchange for my life.*'

He could, of course, sell his assets, he told Susanne, but it wouldn't be enough to satisfy the demands that were being made of him.

Susanne was shocked. For a moment caution – deeply embedded caution – controlled her response. She held him tight: he was to boast much later that she held him like a mother clutching a child. She told him that he must somehow try to tackle this as best he could. It was his responsibility to do so. And, then something struck her ...

'*Just how did you manage to leave the United States with such a serious charge hanging over you?*' she asked carefully.

Helg was ready for that question. He was ready for any question. '*I have two passports, a Swiss passport and a diplomatic one. I used the diplomatic passport – immunity, no questions asked, you know the kind of thing – and I am now faced with finding the necessary money.*'

Despite her love for him (or was it infatuation now?), there was something about the story that worried her. She couldn't put her finger on what it was ... Helg had mentioned the life-threatening position he now found himself in, yet he hadn't gone into any real detail about what had happened. Surely someone who was in so much trouble would have wanted to talk endlessly about it to find some kind of resolution?

Another matter was to cause her great concern.

As she was preparing to leave the hotel, she mentioned in passing that she had not parked in the hotel's underground car park, in a space that had been provided to Helg for her when he had checked in, as they had previously agreed.

'*Why didn't you park there, when you said you would?*' he exclaimed – and there was such an undercurrent to this tone that she was greatly disturbed. Obvious tension had spread across his face. As she made her way to her car, Susanne's mind was filled with questions – *why hadn't he spoken more of his desperate plight involving the Mafia? And why had he been so angry when she confessed that she had innocently parked somewhere other than the space he had allocated to her?* It made her wonder …

Police investigating later were to wonder if Helg's reaction was caused by the fact that Ernani Barretta lay in wait in the underground car park, video-camera at the ready, to film the couple as Helg escorted Susanne down to her car. With her vehicle parked elsewhere, there was no way for Ernani to know that Susanne had even left the hotel. The whole operation, which would have entailed luring Susanne to the out-of-town hotel, revealing the Mafia–child story to her and getting video shots of her walking to Helg's parking place, had blown up in their faces, all thanks to a simple unexpected decision by the victim.

Susanne headed back to her sheltered villa, to her husband and her children, a little confused, but still largely smitten by Helg. Over the following days, in between the demands of her role at the head of BMW and her associated company duties, she went over the scene in the Tulip Inn, time and time again. She applied a clinical, psychological approach to her examination of the rendezvous. The basic question she came back to was the same one that she usually asked when she met someone interested in befriending her: *is he or she after my money?*

Was that really how it was with Helg? *No.* He hadn't actually asked her for money. He hadn't actually asked for her help in any way. He'd simply told her about that terrible accident in the United States. And the consequences.

Who else could he relate such a terrifying story to, if not to someone he loved? It was only natural for him to want to sound her out about this dreadful event. They had made love several times now but their relationship was based on their intimate chats and shared desires. Yet, she had shown indifference to his plight, to his need for financial help, even though he had actually not come right out and asked for it. Perhaps, she considered, she had been too dismissive.

Slowly, as the days passed, Susanne realized that she needed to hear more about what had happened in Miami. Hitting a Mafia child in a car accident, being threatened with personal harm if he didn't pay compensation on top of any insurance, escaping to Switzerland with his diplomatic passport … it sounded so completely implausible taken as a whole, yet there was no hint that Helg was conning her. In fact, he had something of a spiritual aura about him, she thought. He was certainly intelligent and he cared about the world as his interest in renewable energies showed. She had to hear more. By now she was coming round to the idea that she was going to help her lover.

She decided not to call him. She would keep it businesslike, if money – *her* money – was to be involved. So, she sent him a fax at a number that he had given her. In essence, she told him that she was considering helping him but before she did so she needed to clarify a few points about the accident.

There could only have been great rejoicing in the Sgarbi–Barretta camp after that fax came through. It is not known whether Helg and Ernani were together at the time, although police suspect that they were. Ernani is alleged to be an essential player in 'Operation Klatten' and the man who acted as the 'film director', keeping a digital record of Helg and Susanne together, wherever possible, with electronic 'spy' devices, just in case the screws needed to be turned. Despite the failed attempt at filming in the Tulip Inn's car park, they already had some evidence of the affair, but they wanted something better. There was an exciting future ahead of them, they agreed, especially as on the face of it, Susanne was coming through. They went over the Mafia story again, making sure they had sewn up any loose ends.

Helg called Susanne.

'*I want to hear your story again before I can help you,*' she told him. '*If it's not as you've told it before, if there's something different, some kind of emergency that you felt you didn't want to share with me, please tell me what it is. Just be honest with me. Tell me exactly what your difficulty is.*'

He did not budge from the story he had originally told her. '*It's just as I explained it – the child, the demands from the Mafia.*'

But she continued to press him for more details.

'*I've told you everything – the rental car in Miami, going too fast, the accident with the little girl, the statement to the police and then a phone call making it quite clear to me that someone very high up in the Mafia was very, very angry that I had left his little girl so seriously injured that she might be a paraplegic.'*

She let his words sink in. Should she be suspicious? Was it just too incredible? On the other hand, he still hadn't asked her for anything.

'What do you want from me?' she asked, although there was an obvious reluctance in her voice. *'Do you need money?'*

She was sure he could pick up on her tone. Instead, he told her that he had not explicitly asked for money because their relationship was not founded on material things, but love. This time his soft words failed to move her, combined with his inability to provide the finer details that she had hoped to hear about the Miami affair.

'I'm sorry,' she said. *'I just have a bad feeling about this entire story. I just don't think I'm going to be able to offer my help.'*

Yet again, she felt bad about questioning him. And, once more, in the solitude of her home, she ran through the entire saga again – both what he had told her in the Tulip Inn and their most recent conversation. *Should she help him? Should she ignore his yet unspoken but nonetheless implied plea for help? If she turned him down, would that be the end of their affair?* Whether their continuing relationship depended on her answer was one of the things she struggled with. She felt awful, as she was to tell the police much later.

'I had failed to help a person who was really in need.'

After several days of further soul-searching she called Helg again. It was by now early September.

'Another opportunity … I want to hear it again. Every detail. I'm sorry to ask again, but I just need to be sure.'

On 6 September, Susanne parked her car in the underground garage of the Holiday Inn and walked purposefully towards the lift. She knew her way by now, having met Helg there a few weeks earlier. As she stepped into the familiar room, Helg wrapped his arms around her. He had been looking forward to this moment for more reasons than one. It is not known whether he embellished his original story before or after they went to bed together but the time came when Susanne asked him to repeat again the specific details about his plight and to spell out just how much money he required to evade the Mafia. He offered her a soft drink – perhaps a 7-Up – from the hotel bar, and then he stunned her, by saying, '*I'm 7 million euros short... It's more than that, in fact. I need 10 million all up, but if I sell my assets I can raise 3 million.*'

Before she could say more, he broke down how the money was to be paid – one third for a firm of lawyers in the States, one third for the girl's parents and the last third, his own special request, to be deposited into a special account for the little girl.

'*She's going to need on-going medical care. There are grave fears that she has been so badly injured she'll be a paraplegic. She's definitely going to need a lot of attention in the coming years and in addition to the insurance this will be my personal contribution towards helping her.*'

The hours slipped by as they hugged and he continued to pour out his grief, the sadness written across his face. And while he spoke of money and how terrible he felt about the accident, she was to realize later that he had still not provided her with precise details about the accident. Where it had happened – the street, the district, the day and time – whether the police had charged him, where he had been staying at the time ... fine details that in retrospect she would have liked to have learned, but from which she had been distracted from asking. He had caressed her while he spoke of dividing up the money and talked about his own pain for the child. His evident emotion quashed the questions that she should have asked.

'*This has weighed very heavily on me,*' he said. '*I've been having bad dreams about it all. I've worked out what I can sell, but it's still not enough – nothing like near enough.*'

He told her that he had already sold his car and his house and had cashed in his investments. But still woefully short, he didn't know what to do now. That was why he had turned to her – not for money but for advice, a shoulder to lean on.

She hugged him again. And in the room next door, thanks to the recording device that he and Helg had set up earlier, Ernani Barretta rubbed his hands with glee. Helg and Susanne were talking money. *Big money.* And what was more, he now had evidence. More images to add to his growing collection. Pictures of his disciple, his rock, making love to one of the wealthiest women on Earth.

THE MULTI-MILLION EUROS '7-UP' PLOT

In their plan to skim millions of euros from the BMW heiress, Helg and Ernani had studied every secret camera device available on the market. The days of drilling holes through walls and framed pictures to record action in an adjoining room were long past. In a high-tech age there were many devices that could be hidden in a hotel room and no-one would be any the wiser. Pictures could be sent wirelessly to a recording device – a computer the best option – in an adjoining room.

There are spy cameras made to look like bedside alarm clocks, small desk-top calculators, mobile phones, a tissue box and even a pen. They are virtually impossible to detect and it is almost 100 percent guaranteed that the unsuspecting victim will be caught on camera doing things that he or she doesn't want others to witness.

★ ★ ★

'*I'll help you,*' she said at last. '*In what form do you need the money?*'

Remaining absolutely calm despite his inner elation, for he was the consummate player in such moments as these, he told Susanne that he needed it in cash because time was vital. He would be paying the money into a Swiss account and he did not want any delays that might occur with an electronic transfer – and it would also be more difficult to trace Susanne as the source of the money.

It was only a loan, she repeated, and he spread his hands – one of his many habitual expressions that suggested 'of course' and which had previously endeared him to so many. He said *that* was understood.

'*I will not only return everything to you – I'll pay you back double. I know how to earn money. It's just that I don't have this kind of amount to pay these people in the time that it must be paid. This is why it's so pressing and why I've been so miserable recently.'*

Having made up her mind to help him, Susanne immediately set about getting the money together. As Helg lay back on the bed, she called Bad Homburg and spoke to Dr Johannes Fritz, director of a company that handled the Quandt family affairs. She told him that she required a large amount of funds because she had decided to help someone.

Helg and Susanne discussed what would happen to the money – twice the original principal – when he returned it. Susanne told him she would donate it to charity.

'I wouldn't want to keep it for myself.'

'I think that's a wonderful idea,' he commented.

Despite the affection that she felt for him, Susanne had switched to a business mode ... of sorts. There were formalities that in other circumstances she would have insisted on, but this time the arrangement was more fluid. However, she did continue to make it clear that this was not a gift. Helg assured her again that he would repay it, but his promise was the only 'security' he could offer – and so she accepted his word. They did not talk of any interest that would accrue, but he did state that it would take a little time for him to refund her, even as much as two or three years, but given the large sum Susanne felt that was a reasonable and relatively short period.

She was to tell authorities later: *'Because I had a relationship with Mr Sgarbi, I felt particularly close to him but I did not wish to become involved in other matters that he was involved in.'* And, in a comment that was to betray all of her vast business knowledge and the many years she had spent in high-powered corporate affairs, she added: *'I had no intention of asking him for a written agreement that would commit him to paying me back.'*

She did not even ask him for a receipt for the money, such was her trust in him.

But there was one condition that she did insist on. Perhaps it was because he had offered her a particular soft drink from hotel mini bars – she insisted that the money she was going to lend him should never be referred to as '7 million euros', instead, she said, they should talk of '7-Up'. She was later to explain that she was not, in fact, referring to the soft drink of the same name but the actual amount of money that she was lending to him; the 'up' was a symbol of sorts, like a 'thumbs-up', to indicate that a portion of the money was to be used for something good, in this case the rehabilitation of the injured child. So, it was agreed. Their secret code whenever the money was discussed would be '7-Up'.

Over the following days they remained in touch by telephone, during which Susanne assured Helg that arrangements were being made to get the money together. On 10 September they met again at the Holiday Inn.

It was to be yet another romantic encounter, one in which every move was carefully recorded. And then, they got down to the serious business of talking about the delivery of the money. The handover would have to be carried out with extreme caution, they both agreed, and the most discreet way, Helg thought, was to use the Holiday Inn underground car park for the meeting. That would avoid Susanne having to ride up in the lift, short distance that it was, with such a large amount of money. Besides which, it would only have to be carried downstairs again and it would be extremely heavy. No. It was far more simple just to hand it over in the car park.

Susanne, along with her financial colleague, Dr Fritz, in Bad Homburg, had done her homework. If the money came in 200 euro bills, it would fit into a cardboard box that could be easily handled. So, they worked out the size of the box first and then calculated the number of bills that would be needed to fill it. It was important, too, they decided, that only one box should be used to avoid difficulties in transportation. Helg had no say in the size of each bill; he was the mere 'collector' after all. The evening before the delivery of the cash, Dr Fritz went to the Quandt family's bank and picked up the money.

The following day a driver, who had travelled from Frankfurt, arrived at Susanne's home in Munich with the carton of money, although he had no idea what the box contained. At the villa, the carton was loaded into Susanne's car and she set off for the Holiday

THE MULTI-MILLION EUROS '7-UP' PLOT

Inn where her lover, the gigolo-cum-extortionist, was patiently waiting. A quick phone call told him that she was on the way.

Helg made his way from the room down to the garage, where he had parked an executive rental car, a black Audi A6. On her arrival, they both glanced around the garage – as far as she could tell they were the only two people in the car park. He opened his car boot; she opened hers and the boxload of money, still in individual plastic wraps, was transferred. In the end, the two of them needed to transfer it, for it weighed close to 40 kilograms.

Helg told Susanne that he needed to hurry to catch a plane to take the money to Switzerland and bank it.

As she returned home, Susanne's mind raced. She went over the entire story again, as he'd told it to her, for such an astonishing series of events is not easily erased from the mind. And other questions now raised their heads: now he had the 7 million euros, how was he going to fly with it to Switzerland? He couldn't put it in the hold, surely? Doubts surfaced. What if …?

But then Helg phoned her. At close to 7p.m. her mobile rang and the relief she felt was unspeakable. She heard him tell her: '*Everything's gone smoothly. I rearranged the money and put it into sports bags.*'

She assumed he had carried them on board but he did not explain how, even packed into sports bags, he had been able to successfully pass the money through the airport X-ray machine without any questions being asked by airport security.

The following day, he continued, he would go to the appointed bank with his lawyer and there would be a phone link-up with the US lawyers representing the Mafia family. Arrangements would then be confirmed as to how the money would be distributed, divided into thirds, just he had told her, and paid into specified bank accounts. What he failed to tell her, and what she did not ask, was the name of the bank involved.

So smitten was Susanne with her lover that all the barriers she had built up over the years seemed to have fallen away. She never could have forseen when she set off for two weeks of rest and relaxation at the Lanserhof that within an extremely short space of time she,

Susanne Klatten, one of the toughest corporate negotiators in the world, would be freely handing over a fortune of her own money to a relative stranger. She had known Helg Sgarbi for just two months, yet she had given him her heart, her body and now a significant part of her personal fortune. No, if anyone had told her that was to happen as she checked into the Lanserhof on that day in July and slipped on her soft, comfortable bathrobe, she would have laughed.

Only Susanne and her husband, Jan, know whether he suspected that she had found a lover. Whether he saw something different in her behaviour, in her mood, is something we can only guess at. There had been moments when husband and wife had been seen out together – at a concert, perhaps, or a high-society dinner – when they appeared to be the very picture of happiness. A photo at a concert shows them leaning into one another as they applaud; another shows them beaming, Susanne in a red outfit – one of her favourite colours - pressed to her husband's side as they attend yet another society event. With such happiness evident in their marriage, perhaps Jan noticed a change in his wife, something that had started before she had even set out for that fortnight in Lanserhof. Perhaps she had felt an immediate bond with Helg? His apparent sadness had certainly made her believe that they had something in common and she let down her guard because he instilled such a feeling of trust in her. Psychologists were to say later that the helplessness Susanne picked up in Helg touched an emotion in her that said: '*Look after him – he's lost.*'

To Susanne's intense relief, Helg did return to Munich. She still had no idea that the bank and accounts in Switzerland were all a figment of Helg's imagination. She had no idea that he had already met with his guru, Ernani Barretta, who on opening the boot of Helg's car, had been heard to exclaim: '*Good God – that's a whole cubic metre of money!*'

What a catch she was – and Ernani and Helg agreed that this was only the beginning. After all, Susanne and Helg had enjoyed liaisons in discreet hotels and she had given herself over to him entirely. She also apparently believed that the relationship was guaranteed to continue for a long time to come because he was committed to repaying the money in full over the next year or so. Helg's apparent sincerity seemed to confirm that she should have no doubts about their future, that he had no intention of letting her go. He wanted her to stay with him, to leave her husband, even start a new life with him, along with the children. It would make not make any difference to his love for her, he had told her.

Now back in Munich he had a proposal to put to her. To make things easier for them both, instead of risky rendezvous in hotel rooms, Helg said that he had signed the contract on an apartment – somewhere to spend time alone together. It would be available at the end of September, he told her. Later that month, however, he informed Susanne that he had to go away again – he'd been called up for an assignment in his role as a 'special adviser'.

His absence was to prove a difficult time for Susanne. Jan noticed something in her behaviour that worried him so much that he asked her straight out: '*Are you having an affair?*'

Susanne had no choice but to lie to him; she told him not to be so concerned. But she knew she was coming to a time soon when the truth would come out, one way or the other. There was far too much at stake – her beautiful home, her marriage and children – everything to lose for the man she had fallen for but whom she, in reality, did not really know. And, there was a nagging 'edge' to him that she could not explain. If truth be told it had always been there.

The villa was filled with tension and Susanne found it increasingly difficult. She decided that she needed some direction – if only she could ask someone she trusted whether she should continue her relationship with Helg and its unknown future, or return to the safe, domestic cocoon that had sheltered her for most of her adult life.

This was all overshadowed temporarily by the nightmare events of the weekend of 29 and 30 September 2007. Without any warning, the documentary about the Quandt family links to the the Nazi regime was aired on German television. And the media clamoured for the family's reaction. A comment from Susanne, as the most prominent member of the Quandts involved in BMW, was demanded by the press. She was, after all, the granddaughter of Günther Quandt, whose battery factories had allegedly caused the deaths of countless slave labourers during the Nazi war years.

If Susanne had wished any time of her life to just go away, it was that weekend.

★ ★ ★

On Helg's fake return from his latest alleged secret assignment – in fact, yet another meeting with Ernani to discuss further tactics – she told him about Jan's suspicions and the stress it was causing her.

Helg repeated his earlier suggestion; that she leave her husband and start a new life with him. While she was thinking about it, he said, she should, at least, consider the apartment he had rented as her 'second home', somewhere they could meet and she could decide on her future.

Again, Susanne agreed to do as he asked and travelled with him to the apartment. It wasn't so far from the Holiday Inn. A short trip along Leopoldstrasse, heading away from the city, and then a right turn at a service station into a small street. Nothing could be more innocuous, particularly for a woman with the corporate and social stature of Susanne Klatten.

They drove into the underground car park and then travelled up to one of the upper floors. A short walk along a corridor and Helg was unlocking the door to their new apartment.

She was shocked.

The place had just two rooms, with cooking facilities in the corner of the main room, and a separate bathroom. Apart from that it was completely empty. If she had imagined a grand apartment in keeping with a man who was involved in mergers and acquisitions and went on secret assignments for the Swiss Government she could not have been more surprised at the sight of this nondescript apartment that was no more than 50 square metres. There were no curtains and the only view out of the window was towards a complex of offices across the street, now filled with workers. She was terrified that they would see her through the uncovered window and that someone might recognize her. She stayed out of sight, sitting on the floor. There was nowhere else.

Helg had told her, she reflected, that he could sell his assets for an estimated 3 million euros and she accepted that he possibly would not have had the time to do so. Even so, it was curious that he had not been able to rent an apartment that was a little more sumptuous. At least, somewhere with furniture. But of greater concern was the fact that the location and situation of the apartment was the very opposite of discreet. It contrasted completely with the almost obsessive need for privacy that he had displayed when meeting her on previous occasions for their romantic trysts.

It would not have even crossed her mind that there was another, far more sinister reason for Helg's choice of that particular apartment, so close to the red-fronted office complex across the street. Anyone in that building – whether there legitimately or otherwise – someone perhaps in an empty office space, could aim a video-camera straight at the apartment and record every movement that the couple made.

Susanne went to the bathroom. Again, this raised questions – why were there no personal items? Not even a toothbrush, a razor, certainly not the after-shave she knew all too well that he used? He had given her the impression earlier that he had already moved in to the place, but now he told her that he had only just rented the apartment and was planning to buy furniture from Ikea. Mention of the popular store, she may have reflected later, was part of the ploy to show that he had not kept back any of her money to splash around.

On her return to the room, she leaned back against the wall, well out of sight of the window. Again, Helg spoke of the future that they might have together. He asked her why she had not told her husband that she had met someone else. He also wanted to know why she hadn't made up her mind to leave Jan and set up home with him.

'I can make this promise to you,' he said. *'While I cannot offer you anything of a financial nature – you know very well my situation on that front – I can be of assistance in helping you to make more money. You know that I'm in M&A [mergers and acquisitions]. I have many contacts there and there's a fund that I believe you should consider investing in.'*

As Susanne sat in stunned silence, Helg went on to describe how the fund he was talking about was extremely healthy, as he had used it just recently for another wealthy customer.

Questions began to fill her mind … questions, always questions. There was not a day since she had met him that she did not have a niggling doubt about one thing or another. And now, when she had just loaned him 7 million euros to get out of his horrible situation, here he was suggesting that she should part with even more cash.

'What kind of money are you talking about?' she still asked.

He gave her a reassuring smile. *'They wouldn't even take your money for anything less than 290 million euro. It's a very, very, serious business concern. You are well aware of the money market. It's pointless in putting peanuts into it.'*

Filled with uncertainty, Susanne pulled herself to her feet. All she said was that she would think about his proposition.

'Just stay calm about what's happening at home,' he told her. *'Think about what we've discussed and let's get back in touch in a few days. I've got to go off on another assignment that's just come up, so we'll speak when I've returned.'*

She drove home, overwhelmed with doubt, yet again. She was on the verge of destroying her marriage – not that it wasn't already on shaky ground. There was no question now in her mind that her affair with Helg, the smooth-talking stranger, to whom she had just passed an inordinate amount of money, would mean the kiss of death to all the years of happiness she had spent with Jan.

She felt trapped. Who could she turn to without Jan finding out? He already had his suspicions. That much was obvious. She concluded there were three options open to her: she would have to sort out everything on her own; she could consult friends and even family members; or she could seek professional help.

Finally she came to a tough decision – '*A moment of clarity,*' she was to say later. '*You are a victim and you have to fight back. Otherwise it will never end.*'

She would have to seek the help of professionals. She simply could not bear the mental torment that she was experiencing any longer.

PART FOUR
The Plot Unravels

BLACKMAIL

At his office in Erdinger Strasse in Aschheim, east of Munich's city centre, Dr Nikolaus Seibt had no hesitation in taking the call that his secretary put through. The balding, bespectacled head of the Institute for Conflict Research and Crisis Counselling knew the caller well: he had spent many hours with Susanne Klatten and her husband in the past, advising them on maintaining their personal safety, given their wealth.

Susanne, it seemed, wanted to see Dr Seibt as a matter of urgency. It was a *personal* matter. He agreed to make his time available to her immediately.

Dr Seibt was a recognized expert in his field; he provided advice to company executives who had much to lose through robbery, kidnapping, embezzlement and blackmail. With 25 years experience in this dangerous field, he was the one man who Susanne Klatten knew she could trust with the crisis that threatened to consume her. He had provided sound advice to companies, executives and their families on how to safeguard against possible threats – and he had also delved into the minds of the people suspected of planning criminal activity. His organization boasted expertise in the fields of threat analysis, assessment of a company's security status and prevention concepts.

Just one year earlier Dr Seibt had given German listeners an insight into some of his security work when he agreed to an interview for Bavarian Radio. He told how his group of experts worked with specialized police units and advised industrial firms during crisis situations. His work involved examining their daily life styles and personal habits, and then coming up with a plan that not only improved their security but allowed them to continue a quality of life.

From an analysis of up to 150 kidnapping cases, Dr Seibt and his team had learned to understand the psychology of abductors – and others in the early stages of planning crimes. He also spoke about blackmail letters and how the language used might help experts read the 'psycho-structure' driving the offender. But he was speaking about those extortionists whose identity was unknown in cases in which a profile had to be built up before the police could move in on the offender.

Susanne Klatten's case was different. When she contacted Dr Seibt she already had the name of her suspected blackmailer she could provide him with. It was the name of her lover.

Susanne poured out her story to Dr Seibt – recalling in detail the meeting with Helg at the Lanserhof spa, the subsequent contacts, the Mafia child accident and the loan of 7 million euros to him. She told him that she was now very worried that her relationship with Helg Sgarbi posed a very real threat to her family. Perhaps she was wrong, she said, and was unfairly judging her lover, but she could not shake off the nagging feelings of doubt about Helg's true intentions.

Immediately after her meeting with the security expert, somewhere around 8 to 10 October 2007, she was to recall, she phoned Helg. She had no idea where he was, but his phone was on.

'*It's over,*' she said. '*I won't be seeing you again.*'

'*What?*' he exclaimed, genuinely shocked. '*What's going on? Are you being forced to make this decision? Do you have a gun pointed at your head?*'

She wasn't going to argue. Following instructions given to her by Dr Seibt, she cut the connection. The matter of the 7 million euros she had handed over was not discussed.

The enormous pressure that Susanne had been under did not go away just like that, however. There were too many loose ends, despite her long conversation with Dr Seibt, and she feared what might happen in the immediate future.

She had been so careful about her security throughout her life, yet she had thrown decades of caution to the wind for a man that she was now finally admitting to herself, she knew next to nothing about – apart from his bedroom technique.

What evidence did she have that he was some kind of 'secret agent' who worked for the Swiss Government, for example? And was there any proof that the Mafia child story was true? She had seen nothing to back up any of his fantastic claims, yet he was asking her to outlay more and more money.

She needed time away to clear her head, to enjoy soothing massages. Make the world go away. Her public relations people were dealing with the problems raised by the TV programme linking the family to the Nazi slave labour factories. But her personal problems remained and she was living a nightmare.

There was one simple answer. She would have to escape for a while … go to a place where she knew she could relax. She packed her bag and headed for the mountains – to the Lanserhof.

On 12 October Susanne checked into the Austrian spa resort. She had refused to take Helg's calls on her mobile and as an added precaution, she had told the reception desk at the Lanserhof that no calls should be put through to her, unless they were from husband. But to her horror, it wasn't long before she learned of one person who had tried repeatedly to contact her there and had left a message for her to call him – Helg Sgarbi.

Who had told him she was there? She was completely unnerved but she clung to the hope that he would eventually give up trying to contact her.

Four days later, she was left reeling.

The receptionist handed her an envelope. She took it to her room and peeled it open. She pushed her fingers in through the flap and began to pull out a series of photographs. Feeling slightly puzzled, she then began to realize what she was looking at: leafing through the pictures, one by one, she recognized first the naked woman. Herself. Enaged in sexual activity with Helg Sgarbi.

There were all kinds of photographs of her – with her clothes on, clothes off. It was all there. She stared at those clothes. Where had these disgusting pictures been taken? She tried to recognize the surroundings. The Holiday Inn, of course. Their very first rendezvous there on 20 or 21 August. So, he'd set her up. Right from the very beginning.

There was nothing accompanying the pictures. But she read the implication all too well and the threat the photographs implied; she feared what would follow next. And when it would happen.

BLACKMAIL

The follow-up blow came 13 days later, on 23 October, when she was back in Munich. A personal fax arrived making reference to the wonderful times the sender and Susanne had had together. The letter was signed by one 'Fatima Lanser'. Susanne immediately recognized the reference – Fatima is one of the characters in the book that she had been reading when she first met Helg at the Lanserhof, *The Alchemist*. 'Lanser', of course, referred to the Lanserhof. But there was some mystery surrounding the actual content of the letter. The language used did not 'sound' like Helg Sgarbi. The German expressions were different to the kind he would use and she suspected that the entire text was either made up of quotes from literature or that the letter had been composed by someone else writing under his instructions.

As the days rolled by the letters and texts continued to arrive. *'Do you remember, my love, when we met in broad daylight in a Munich hotel room after your holidays …?'*

Police were later to come into possession of a love letter written by Helg that spoke of lust and passion, although it was not revealed if it was addressed to Susanne. It read: *'Do you remember how we fused in lust on the beach and you groaned loudly with passion?'* But in another letter that was addressed to Susanne, Helg signed off as *'Your gentle warrior'*.

Hoping to persuade him to think again about what he was doing, Susanne began taking his calls. Unlike in the past though, it was quickly evident that things had changed – there was no love in his tone. He wanted '7 times 7-Up.' He was asking for 49 million euros.

She went back to her security adviser, Dr Seibt. His advice to her to cut off the relationship immediately had been sound, but by then it was already too late. The sex tapes were already in Helg's hands, ready to be used should she refuse to co-operate with his demands for more money.

Dr Seibt did not hesitate in making his next decision. He took Susanne to the Bavarian Landeskriminalamt (LKA), the state police headquarters. With Dr Seibt at her side, Susanne met senior officers there and told them everything – and to back up her statement, she showed them the original fax she had received and the text messages.

Given the profile of Susanne Klatten and the fact that blackmail is an extremely serious crime, the police treated the complaint as a matter of the highest priority. Technicians were called in and from that time on, every call that Helg Sgarbi made to Susanne was recorded.

The police file on the case built up quickly. In the following weeks, Helg was heard by officers listening into his calls to Susanne, insisting on receiving the '7 times 7-Up', failing which he would send intimate photos to every member of her family, as well as the members of all the boards of the companies on which she sat. The photos he had sent her, he said, were just a taster. He also had videos of her with him and they were so good that he became sexually excited just watching them. Just imagine what her husband would think, he warned. He had also kept all the SMS messages that she had sent him. And he was in possession of all her love letters in which she allegedly told him that they were *twin souls*. He had a record of every moment, every word, every move and worse, every intimacy, of their affair.

Her tormentor tried to justify his actions by claiming in a phone call that she had broken his heart and left him in a deep spiritual crisis. She had ruined his life and it was time for her to return 'the favour'. He insisted his demands were not blackmail, just mere justice.

Then he spoke of atonement – atonement for what he claimed she had done to him? Or perhaps for the sins of her ancestors? By now the revelations about the Quandt family had been aired on TV and the claims that the documentary had made were followed up in newspapers and magazines across Europe. Helg told Ernani that his Polish–Jewish grandfather had been one of the workers who had suffered in the Quandt's munitions factories during the war.

If he truly believed that his relative had suffered under Susanne's grandfather, his cruel plan to set her up and extract money from her would have given him extreme satisfaction – he was exacting some kind of revenge on his grandfather's behalf. In such circumstances, when he made love to her and listened to her speak of her feelings for him, it would be surprising if he had not found it difficult to suppress a smile of victory at being able to extract a fortune from the woman whom he saw as living off the proceeds of those cruel Nazi factories.

Helg's demands on Susanne became a combination of everything that he could throw at her, but the end result was the same – he was making threats to extort an enormous sum of money from her. Along with the threats came mockery – she and her husband had their 'horns up' against one another, he said, and she had destroyed the dignity of her children by sneaking away from her family to enjoy an affair with him. Such words, analysts were to agree, were the actions of a 'psycho-terrorist', a man who knew how to thrust the knife in and then slowly twist it, while mockingly laughing.

By delaying delivery of the money that he was asking for, Helg told Susanne in a letter, she was placing herself at very high risk, whereas his own were 'irrelevant'. She stood to lose far more than he would. He would tell the world everything. He would even put the videos and the photos on the internet. Her reputation would be destroyed.

He sent her another package. A video. More photos. The police needed to see them this time. She spared herself her blushes and handed them over; then she listened to their instructions.

When Helg's next telephone demand came, his voice showing obvious impatience, Susanne told him that it was impossible for her to raise the '7 times 7-Up' for security reasons. Her bankers just wouldn't allow that kind of money to be withdrawn without asking questions about where it was going to. To ask for it in cash, she told Helg, simply added to the problem.

'I'll take 2 times 7-Up, then,' he finally agreed.

Fourteen million euros.

But even that would take time now to get together, she said. It would have to be after Christmas, early in the new year. She would tell him when and where.

'*No!*', he exclaimed.

She was in no position to be dictating the terms. He would make the arrangements. The handover would not be in Germany. He wasn't going to trust her and her German friends. They would speak later about what the final arrangements would be.

Susanne put the phone down and turned to the police officers who had been monitoring the call. They nodded. She had done very well.

Helg hung up, then he dialled a new number. When it was answered, he said: '*Ernani, she's going to pay 14 million!*'

THE FINAL RENDEZVOUS

Only Susanne and her mild-mannered husband, Jan, would be able to tell the world of the scenes that took place in their luxury Munich home when she confessed everything to him. But the long-held rules of privacy that had controlled them through their marriage ensured that nothing was made public about their personal relationship.

Jan had had his suspicions that she had been having an affair. He had seen her telephone bill with numbers on it that he did not recognize at a time that coincided with a marked change in her behaviour. He still needed to hear it from Susanne, though, and her confession to him could have come only amid a flood of tears.

Now the air was clear. She'd owned up to everything to her security adviser, to the police and, most importantly, to her husband. It would now be up to the police to do their work and bring this terrible episode in her life to its inevitable conclusion.

Any woman duped in the way that she had been would have subsequently gone over events time and again.

What was it about Helg that had allowed her defences to crumble? Yes, there was the bond that she had felt between them, the shared spirituality, the loneliness, it was true. On his side, though, it had all been a sham.

Why hadn't she seen that? Why hadn't she realized that his sadness, the same sadness that had stirred in her a feeling that they had something in common, was nothing more than a role played by a skilful actor? Perhaps, she told herself, it was because the setting had been so perfect, for who would have believed that a con man would have chosen to strike in the calm surroundings of the Lanserhof? It was so unlikely. Then again, she was becoming increasingly convinced that he must have *known* she would be there.

THE FINAL RENDEZVOUS

In any case, in such tranquil surroundings her protective barrier had been down. He had subtly wormed his way into her affections, appearing to talk about spiritual things and then following it up by clever stories of secret missions with just a glamorous hint of danger, and then he'd capped it all by being enchanting, telling her enthralling accounts of his travels to the Middle East, of his own search for spirituality in those Biblical lands. He had quite simply fascinated her. He had led her along so well that even their strolls down to the village near the resort and their casual walks through the nearby valleys had failed to satisfy her curiosity. That was why she had fallen for him.

Susanne would have blamed herself, but she might also have found another excuse for her behaviour, for she was not alone. There have been many cases of wealthy women falling into the hands of clever conmen. In the 1970s, the extremely wealthy Christina Onassis, daughter of shipping tycoon Aristotle Onassis, with a personal fortune of US $500 million, fell prey to a procession of playboys, all of them after her money. Her second husband, Alexander, along with his mother, demanded US $20 million from her within the first six months of her marriage. When that marriage ended, she had a disastrous third marriage, before taking a fourth husband, Thierry Roussel, a French playboy who had once been described as the world's most successful gigolo. He persuaded her to pay him US $30 million to compensate him for the inconvenience of moving him to Switzerland to be with her. Eventually, having taken a fortune from her, he sought a divorce. With nobody she could trust around, Christina was easy prey for conmen looking to make a fast buck and she lost many millions to fraudsters. In 1988, she was found dead in a bath, officially succumbing to pulmonary edema, but many people believed that an overdose of barbiturates was the true cause of her death.

Another playboy-cum-gigolo who made a fortune from the women he bedded was Dominican diplomat, polo player and racing car driver Porfirio Rubirosa Ariza who was linked with such famous and beautiful women as Eartha Kitt, Ava Gardner, Rita Hayworth, Zsa Zsa Gabor, Veronica Lake and Eva Peron. He married two of the world's richest women, Barbara Hutton and Doris Duke, but it was also claimed that when money became scarce – if that was ever possible with such a supply – he resorted to stealing jewellery and becoming involved in fraudulent schemes.

Whether she was aware of these disturbing tales, Susanne had been well briefed to be on her guard at all times. But a glimpse of a different kind of world can be a tempting escape from years of relative seclusion and now, as she struggled to come to terms with the knowledge that she had been well and truly scammed, along with the very serious threat to her marriage and her reputation, she may have considered that she had paid a high price for grasping at freedom.

But one thought – aside from the stark reality of possibly destroying her family – helped her through the crisis. In coming forward as she had, she was making a stand, not only for herself, but for all the other women facing the same kind of threat from playboys determined to extort their money from them.

While Susanne and her family hoped that the affair could be covered up, she had been warned that if arrests followed that her name might leak out to the press, one way or another. She had to be prepared for that. She was going to need enormous courage, it seemed, but her advisers could already see that she possessed that. She'd already shown it by going to the police.

First and foremost in her mind was her family. According to police sources, she and her husband, along with other family members, met at the Quandt villa in Bad Homburg for a crisis meeting. There were concerns that the shock of learning about Susanne's affair and her decision to extract 7 million euro from the family trust might be too much for the 82-year-old matriarch, Johanna.

Johanna, affectionately known as the Queen Mother among BMW employees, would most probably have had one of two responses – compassion for her daughter who had been so cruelly duped; or utter fury that she could have so wickedly betrayed her husband, her entire family and placed in peril the good name of the company. Perhaps, in the end, it was a mixture of both but it would be surprising if many tears did not flow that day, particularly Susanne's as she tried to gently explain what had happened and why she had fallen for the man she had now learned from police was an experienced gigolo, who had smooth-talked and threatened other wealthy women out of their money.

The one good thing out of this, she explained, was that plans were afoot to catch him red-handed and put an end to the misery he had brought and was bringing to other wealthy women across Europe.

But things had to change, the family agreed, according to intimate sources. There would be no more withdrawals of large funds owned by the family company without the consent of all other members. Withdrawals would no longer be handled by a single director alone.

★ ★ ★

It is a relatively easy, but boring 700km (435 miles) drive from Munich to Pescosansonesco; it is autostrasse for most of the way, but flying and then picking up a rental car would cut the travelling time to just a couple of hours – 52 minutes to Rome airport and a couple of hours drive to Ernani's village.

Whatever means of travel he chose, Helg was there, at the Rifugio Valle Grande. Late afternoons during the period that he was sending his blackmail letters and pictures to Susanne, would find Helg enjoying a glass of wine with the man describing himself as 'God's Personal Messenger'. And in the evening, over a plate of pasta personally cooked by Ernani himself – for everyone who had tasted his food agreed that he was the 'master of pasta' – they could be seen discussing their latest money-making mission.

In all the history of his various seductions, nothing compared to his conquest of Susanne Klatten, Helg agreed with Ernani as they touched glasses. It was all so unbelievable, Ernani admitted, even though he had been well aware of what had been going on, the silent witness to the entire affair. Yet, with the arrival of each bag full of money, he still gloated like a child receiving a new toy.

If truth be told, he had acquired a number of new 'toys' and they were parked out in the forecourt and in his garages – 10 luxury vehicles, including a Rolls Royce Silver Shadow, a Lamborghini Diablo and a Ferrari. Then there were the 'cheaper' vehicles, the four Mercedes, the Audi Q7, a Toyota and one other limousine. There were no BMWs, though. Ernani had 'laundered' a portion of the money Helg had brought him by purchasing motor vehicles, along with investing in a burgeoning empire of real estate in and around Pescosansonesco.

He was particularly fond of two villas he had purchased in the swish northeast tourist resort of Corvara, under the shadow of Mount Sassongher, at the higher end of the Val Badia valley. With the Dolomites surrounding the village, it was a sought-after ski resort. There was more. Ernani had also purchased land in Corvara and Pescosansonesco. Then there was the home he had bought in Torre de Passeri, a few kilometres from his country house.

Aside from the money Helg had brought to him, there was also the small fortune he had amassed from his devoted followers, many of whom were still working without pay in the restaurant area of his complex and keeping the gardens in order. Police were to claim that an elderly Zurich woman had also signed over all her assets to Ernani and had died without a euro to her name.

After dinner, as Christmas approached, Ernani and Helg sat in the Italian's private quarters, a warm, comfortable lounge room with a tiled floor, wood-panelled walls, a floral-decorated lounge suite and bright red drapes at the window. A powerful telescope was aimed at the winter sky. Susanne Klatten, their most recent catch would be the last for a while, they agreed, although Helg told his guru that he still had one or two other ladies in his sights. But for the time being those victims were not worth wasting time over because Susanne would have no choice but to keep them for the foreseeable future.

They discussed the various risks. Would the BMW heiress go to the authorities?

Impossible. She had far too much to lose.

Would she *dare* risk her marriage and the good name of her company for the sake of a few million euros?

No, they agreed, *she would not*.

THE FINAL RENDEZVOUS

The money was a mere drop in the ocean of her enormous wealth. So, they proceeded with their plan to collect the '2 times 7-Up', the 14 million euros that she had agreed to pay for Helg's silence.

To make things a little more difficult legally, should anything go wrong, they decided that the rendezvous would be in a neutral country, one other than their own and that of Susanne. Austria was the best bet, they agreed. They would find a location, an assembly point, that was an easy drive for her from Munich and one which they could also reach in a reasonable time from Zurich. Then Helg would contact Susanne again and give her the instructions that she was waiting for.

The money that Helg had earned so far had been well invested, Ernani told his favourite disciple. He was looking at purchasing further property in Sharm al-Sheikh, a luxury tourist resort on Egypt's Sinai peninsula. He had been captivated by the alluring descriptions in brochures that told how '*all around are Bedouins, colourful tents, mountains and sea.*'

One brochure spoke of all the amenities that could be expected in a tourist region, including casinos, discos, nightclubs, golf courses and health facilities. There were water sports – diving and snorkelling – while inland there were attractions such as desert safaris, camel riding and an array of antiquities to point a camera at. It was ripe for development and Ernani Barretta had the money to spend. None of it was in a bank. He had hidden stashes of it in secret places within easy reach but out of sight of anyone who might come prying.

Ernani often said he did not like to take chances, although he had overlooked the fact that he had been taking them all of his life.

★ ★ ★

As the two men were plotting their next move, telephones were ringing in Germany between the State Investigation Bureau in Munich and the Ministry of the Interior. Messages were being sent via internal emails, each containing the two names that the same man used: *Helg Sgarbi* and *Helg Russak*. Crime analysts held meetings long into the night, reading through a statement Susanne Klatten had provided, along with the threatening letters.

The role of the LKA, as the investigation bureau is known, is to co-ordinate operations to prevent serious criminal activity such as organized crime, drug-trafficking, and terrorist threat. Part of a network of European police bureau, the LKA are experts in crime analysis, but they also have a highly-trained SWAT-style team, the *Spezialeinsatzkommando*, who are called in to deal with hostage dramas, blackmail and bomb threats, among other things.

Police forces in Italy, Switzerland, Austria and France were alerted to be on standby, for until the call came from Helg no-one knew exactly where he had chosen as the drop-off location for the 14 million euros.

When her phone rang Susanne knew she had to remain calm; that she couldn't give him any reason to suspect from her tone, voice or words that the call was being overheard by police.

Was she able to get the money …? Yes. *Was she ready to travel, to set off without raising any suspicion about her whereabouts …?* Yes. *Did she remember Vomp, a few kilometres east of the turnoff to Lanserhof …?* Yes. *And the rest stop there, did she know it …?* Yes, she knew the one he meant.

She was to meet him in the car park and they would make the transfer of what would this time be *two* heavy boxes. The deadline for the transfer was 15 January, but it would be advisable, he told her, if she did not leave things to the very last minute. The day and time was thus set. She added a touch of sadness to her voice as she told him that she would be there in her usual car.

Everything was in place, it seemed. He was going to get his money, he thought. And the police were going to get their man, they knew.

★ ★ ★

This was no normal operation for the highway patrol or a corps of city officers. Cobra, the most skilful commando team in the country was required for this operation.

THE FINAL RENDEZVOUS

Consisting of just a few hundred commandos they had been involved in the 1975 OPEC siege led by the infamous Carlos the Jackal and could claim to be the only counter-terrorism unit that had brought a hijacking to an end while an aircraft was still flying. In that incident, four Cobra officers on board an Aeroflot plane overcame a hijacker who threatened the cockpit crew with a knife.

On 14 January 2008, members of Cobra found themselves airborne again, this time in a helicopter. They were following two cars, a white Audi Q7 and an olive green Mercedes, tracking them as the vehicles crossed the Swiss border into Austria and continued east along the autobahn.

Many kilometres away, commandos in plain clothes, dressed like the many skiers who were heading towards the slopes, lingered in the car park of the Rosenberger rest stop at Vomp. In their unmarked police vehicles were international arrest warrants and the weapons they would use for the men's apprehension. There had been no suggestion at all that Helg Sgarbi or Ernani Barretta were dangerous men physically, despite claims that Ernani really did have links to the Mafia. But, they were taking absolutely no chances.

It was overcast and cold – around 2°C (36.6°F) – but no snow was falling as the two vehicles turned into the car park. They were a little ahead of time. Ernani went into the restaurant to buy a snack and then returned to the Audi, parked just a short distance from Helg's Merc.

And that was when the men from Cobra struck. The doors of Helg's and Ernani's vehicles were flung open simultaneously. Guns were shoved in their faces. Handcuffs snapped on.

There was no Susanne in sight.

Two search teams went through the contents of the vehicles. The boot of Ernani's car was empty, apart from a small bag of overnight clothes. The space had been left for receipt of the two heavy boxes of euros that the two men had expected to collect. But inside the Audi the police found an interesting piece of paper. On it was written the name 'Susanne Klatten', along with her personal mobile phone number. The names of three other women that Helg had scammed were also there, along with their phone numbers.

ﾟ

The Rosenberger rest stop is a clean, efficiently run establishment, part of a national chain, where the waitresses wear brown-and-white check aprons and a vast array of foods, including fruit, are available. Tourist buses, many of them on the way from Munich to Zurich, stop by, the passengers spilling out to stretch their legs, take a photo, drink a coffee. The autobahn traffic rushes past within sight and sound. There is parking in front of the main doors and a larger parking area off to the side. This is where the exchange was to have taken place, away from the eyes of the curious.

'It was very efficiently done,' says a source close to the restaurant chain. 'The management had been warned beforehand that there was to be a police operation and that things had to proceed as normal. So, the tourists came and went. It was assumed that with the two men parking some distance from the entrance there would be no problems regarding public safety and we've since heard that there was no trouble from either of the two men. It was bitterly cold that afternoon so no-one was out wandering around.'

The manager is asked to describe the incident. A message comes back. He does not admit it, but he has been warned – there is to be absolutely no comment to anyone. The implications are clear. No-one talks about a high profile woman like Susanne Klatten.

Why, half the cars in the parking lots are BMWs …

ﾟ

Helg was extradited to Germany, where the original blackmail demands had been made. He had no hope of receiving bail and was locked away in an underground prison in Munich. He made no statement. He said nothing at all, despite the questions that were fired at him. His silence was golden. And the Austrian police were in no position to question Ernani, for the Italian authorities were insisting on dealing with him, as he was one of their citizens.

Despite intense international consultations, the Italian authorities refused to allow the Germans or the Austrians to lay charges against

THE FINAL RENDEZVOUS

Ernani, but they promised he would not be allowed to slip off the hook if evidence of criminal activity could be found. It might take time, but Ernani would be thoroughly investigated.

Ernani may have breathed more than one sigh of relief when senior Cobra officers told him he was free to return to Italy.

As he sped back to Pescosansonesco, the boot of his Audi empty, except for that small bag of clothes with which he'd arrived, he could not believe his good fortune.

When he'd been grabbed he was certain he'd be sharing a prison cell with Helg that night. He resolved to help his friend in whatever way he could, of course, but as for the matter of his having engaged in any kind of crime with the man, he would deny everything. Whatever Helg had got up to was his own problem.

And, didn't Helg tell him that the only reason he'd played tough with Susanne Klatten was in revenge for the treatment his grandfather had suffered in one of the Quandt family factories during the war? That was what Helg had told him; he was sure of that. In any case, that is what Ernani would tell the authorities. It would distance him from any suspicion that he, a simple restaurant owner from the mountains of Italy far, far away, had been working with a smooth-talking gigolo from the big city to rob rich women of their money. Yes, that is what he would tell the police, he decided, as he sped through a series of tunnels near Pescara should they ever came knocking on his door.

To his huge relief, there were no police cars waiting at the gates of the Rifugio Valle Grande when he arrived back at Pescosansonesco late that night. He drove in through the wrought-iron gates, onto the tiled driveway, parked the Audi in the garage, went into the lounge and pouring himself a large glass of his favourite wine, he wondered what the future held.

WHERE IS THE MONEY?

Nicholas Zupo picked up the sheaf of documents that had been sent to him by Austrian police through Eurojust, the EU organization set up by member states in 2002 to fight serious international organized crime. As head of the the Italian mobile police squad in the Adriatic city of Pescara, the handsome, grey-haired commandante had handled numerous cases involving murder, extortion, illegal immigration and anti-drug operations in the past, but he realized that he had now potentially landed one of the most sensational cases of his career.

He knew of Ernani Barretta, the owner of the restaurant and hotel complex in Pescosansonesco, the reputed leader of a strange religious cult whose members never spoke to the people of the village if they could avoid it. He'd heard all kinds of stories about them, as had the local mayor and other town officials. The cult members had been ordered not to speak to each other without the permission of Barretta. In the evenings they ate in silence by candlelight, toiling by day around the property for absolutely no money, so Zupo had heard.

But the topic most discussed by the villagers was the good fortune that seemed to have come Ernani's way. The older folk remembered him from the days when he was just a ragged-clothed kid running with the other poor children of the village. His parents were 'good people', but they had very little money, like so many others in the region. It had been expected that Ernani would continue the Barretta 'line', working away, making what money he could, raising a family, then dying of old age with nothing much to leave behind.

But, all the talk these days was about Ernani's enormous wealth, to the point that he was now known as the 'Prince of Pescosansonesco'. He had set up that incredible Rifugio Valle Grande estate up in the mountains and just look at all the cars that came and went! *All his*! On one occasion he is alleged to have bought one of his limousines locally by handing over a bag full of cash, paying for the vehicle outright. The same, it was whispered, of the houses that he was acquiring in and around the area. All cash buys. But where had the money come from?

From the documents that Zupo was now poring over the answer was becoming quite clear. The man the Germans were holding had been the provider, wooing and threatening great sums of money out of wealthy but vulnerable women – but clever, careful women at that. He must be quite something this Helg Sgarbi, Zupo decided.

The commandante drove around to the office of Gennaro Varone, the Pescara public prosecutor. Varone had received the same documentation as Zupo and it was clear that the Germans expected the Italian authorities to play their part in closing down Ernani's operation and throwing him into prison. They might have lost their major player when Ernani had been allowed to go free, leaving him loose to continue raising money for himself as the self-imposed Messenger of God and the Germans were not happy about that.

However, the German and Austrian authorities had provided the first piece of evidence of an association between Helg Sgarbi and Ernani Barretta – not just in establishing that while Helg and Susanne were in room 629 at the Holiday Inn, Ernani had been occupying 630, the room next door. That *had* to be more than a coincidence. But there was the moment of the arrest at the rest stop at Vomp, where Helg had arranged to meet with Susanne – *again* it had to be more than mere coincidence that Ernani had travelled in convoy with Helg there and was waiting in the car park with him. And then there was the matter of what Ernani was doing with the names and telephone numbers of Helg's targeted victims in his car. *Another* coincidence? There was also the fact that at around the time all those women were being seduced by Helg Sgarbi and he was collecting his blackmail loot, Ernani Barretta began to spend a large amount of money, all in cash, in and around his immediate neighbourhood.

Despite all this initial evidence, Zupo and Varone agreed that the case that had been presented to them was not open and shut. Much was circumstantial. The first difficulty they had to overcome was a legal point, as flagged by lawyers working with Eurojust. The two men suspected of being involved in extorting a fortune from Susanne Klatten were of different nationalities and the crime, therefore, embraced several countries. The stalking of Susanne had apparently begun in Austria and was conducted by a Swiss citizen. It continued in France and while the blackmail demand had been made in Germany, the collection point was in Austria. Complicating matters further was the fact that the proceeds had allegedly been enjoyed by Ernani Barretta and members of his family, who all lived in Italy. The prosecutor explained to Zupo that, as a Swiss citizen, Sgarbi could not be tried in Italy and any proceedings brought against Ernani would have to be in his own country.

A stronger case therefore needed to be built up against Ernani Barretta: hard proof of his involvement in the crimes was key to his conviction. And certainly, it was clear that the funds that Helg had collected from these poor women were not sitting in an Italian bank account somewhere. The money would be far too easy to trace, a fact that they knew Ernani was aware of.

Calculating what they knew was missing, there were at least 10 million euros to be accounted for – and that excluded any funds that Helg might have extorted from other women who had not come forward during the investigation. That was made up of the 7 million euros from Susanne, the 2 million euros that were still owed to the late Comtesse Verena and the funds from the other women, 'G' and 'H'.

'*We need to find how the money has been spent and, if there's any left over, where it is,*' Varone said. '*The obvious question for which we need proof, is: Where has all this money Barretta's been spending come from? It's impossible for him to have earned this much through his business. We know he's been spending big, but there has to be more somewhere. He's not going to tell us, so let's hear what he's got to say on the telephone.*'

Varone said he would arrange for the police to tap Ernani Barretta's telephones. The Rifugio Valle Grande would also be put under police surveillance. That would give them the basics to work with, allowing them to swing into action, when necessary. Further, Varone said he would issue a Letter Rogatory – a formal letter of request from one country's judicial authorities to that in another – asking for assistance to investigate any bank accounts essential to the investigation should details become available to the officers in Italy.

In the meantime, Varone also ordered the seizure of all bank accounts held by Ernani and his family in Italy, until such time as the 7 million euros from Susanne Klatten was found. Particularly targeted, alongside Ernani, would be his wife, Beatrice, his adult children, Clelia and Marcello, and Helg's wife, Gabriele.

Pescara Judge Maria Gabrielle Tascone issued the order to freeze these accounts on the grounds that any funds held in and around the grounds of the country house were allegedly linked to fraud and to the recycling and reuse of the cash proceeds from criminal activity.

In the following weeks, Zupo and Varone, in conjunction with their teams, pulled together every piece of information they could gather about Ernani, his family and what went on behind the iron gates of Rifugio Valle Grande.

On the face of it, the hotel–restaurant complex was a splendid place in which to relax. It was a centre for religious contemplation, for among those who had stayed there were bishops and monsignors of the Catholic Church. Business groups travelled great distances to hold meetings in the conference centre and couples came from far and wide to be married there, spending their first night in one of the rooms, in a large bed with a decorated canopy. Should they wish to have a guided tour around the neighbourhood, there were a number of limousines available, one of which was chauffeured by Ernani's son, Marcello. And the food … well, guests agreed, it was superb!

But, officials studying the complex had also learned from former members of Ernani's cult that behind the religious front lay something different – exploitation, abuse and sexual malice. Many of the women who gathered there to worship – not God, but God's messenger in the form of Ernani – came from troubled backgrounds and were easily led – to Ernani's bed, in most cases, police were told. His 60-year-old wife, Beatrice, it appeared, was complicit, accepting what went on.

It was not an easy place to keep under surveillance for the road leading to the gates was steep and narrow and even the main road below provided no place to hide for a police car. Nevertheless, occasional drives by helped police draw up a picture of daily life at the country house. Undercover officers drove past the gates, surveying the staff – many of them members of Ernani's flock – and watched as, at times, 31-year-old Marcello, Ernani's son, came and went in one of the luxury vehicles.

A sophisticated telephone tapping operation was set up and police officers listened to every conversation that Ernani had, both on the estate's landline and Ernani's mobile. They were convinced that he would make a mistake soon …

★ ★ ★

When he arrived home after Helg's arrest in Austria, Ernani was concerned that he may have been let off the hook too easily. The police could come charging through the doors to his villa at any time. It was essential that they found nothing that could link him back to Susanne Klatten. As for his relationship with Helg, well, they were just good friends, after all.

In the days that followed his return to Pescosansonesco, Ernani set about destroying any evidence of his connection to the blackmail plot. According to police sources he 'vaporized' computer discs containing images of Susanne and Helg together and destroyed print-outs of messages that had been exchanged between the two of them. While the images and the documents had been gathered to help extort millions from the victim and had served Ernani and Helg well, they were now highly dangerous items for Ernani Barretta to be found in possession of. There was still a large amount of cash around, but he had taken care of that.

What he had not taken into consideration, it seemed, was the possibility that the police were monitoring his phone calls. Many of the calls that went out from and were received by Ernani were fairly innocuous, but there were others that left police in no doubt that they were gaining evidence that put Ernani right into the blackmailing frame.

WHERE IS THE MONEY?

In one phone conversation to an undisclosed person, Ernani spoke of being under pressure from Gabriele, Helg's wife, who was pleading with him to '*return the money*'. She had been crying and had begged him to send the money back, he told the listener. Ernani added that she was accusing him of wanting to leave her husband in jail. This, police concluded, was evidence of a financial link between Helg Sgarbi and Ernani Barretta, but they still needed more evidence than that if they were to take proper action against him. Patience was needed and hour-upon-hour of phone calls were monitored.

In another call, police records noted, Ernani had told a male listener that he had already spent at least 2 million euros. There were enough hints in that conversation for police to establish that Ernani had bought two cars valued at 110,000 euros and that he had also purchased a building in Cimone, paid for in cash with banknotes that had originated in Germany.

Despite Helg's many affairs and his own wife's alleged sexual relationship with Ernani, Gabriele was desperate to secure her husband's release from prison, if only on bail. So far, the mobile police squad had heard nothing in her phone conversations that linked either Gabriele or Ernani directly to the intended blackmail of Susanne Klatten, but evidence was to come their way of what they were to describe as a 'criminal association'. In one of her phone calls to an unidentified listener, Gabriele allegedly threatened to cause further grief to the woman who had put her husband behind bars unless she withdrew the charges; she was, she said, in possession of a great deal of evidence that could harm the woman, who police surmised could only be Susanne.

Gabriele also put alleged pressure on Ernani's wife, Beatrice, to persuade her husband to return the money. As police listened in, Beatrice was heard discussing with her husband the possibility of returning the cash in the hope that would result in Helg's release from prison. This conversation left police with only one conclusion – that Beatrice was well aware of the source of her husband's money.

From the flurry of telephone calls police concluded that a number of people associated with Ernani were aware of the Swiss gigolo and the money he had extracted from Susanne. Commandante Zupo was more than pleased with the evidence that his men were collating.

In his further meetings with Prosecutor Verone he reported that he believed Ernani, along with at least one family member, was planning an overseas trip — and intending to take a large sum of money with them. Their investigations of bank accounts in Italy, carried out with the warrants issued by Judge Tascone, had turned up nothing suspicious: Ernani's money was mostly income generated by his restaurant. But that did not come as a surprise to the investigating officers. Police were convinced that the money was in one of three places — tied up in his collection of cars and homes; abroad, where it had been moved to other countries in cash with the help of a number of couriers; or it was located in secret caches that were located in places that only he, and possibly a handful of trusted accomplices, were aware of.

The foreign hideaways for the cash might well have included Switzerland, where the banking system made it extremely difficult, if not impossible, for police to look into individual accounts. The foreign investments, police suspected, might also have been in Egypt, where Ernani was known to be interested in buying property, and also in Croatia, which was within easy flying distance and which was now a popular holiday destination for Italians.

As for the money, analysts agreed that Ernani's only option would have been to hide it — literally bury it, like a pirate's treasure. This was confirmed in a conversation that Ernani had with one of his associates. Ernani complained that, on one occasion, when he recovered a buried can containing 300,000 euros, the notes were 'all wet' and he, therefore, had to ensure that they were buried in a much drier place.

The wiretaps helped police establish the roles that each member of the immediate Barretta family and their associates played in the scams. From their eavesdropping it appeared that at least 10 people knew of the '7-Up' plot and also of the other extortions that had taken place and there was now no question in their minds that Ernani was the co-ordinator of it all. It was also clear that he had made every attempt to ensure that investigators would find nothing incriminating on the estate should they carry out a raid. References to money also led police to conclude that large amounts of cash were, indeed, hidden in and around Rifugio Valle Grande.

Armed with scores of documents containing transcripts of various phone conversations, all that the police squad needed now was a proper trigger in order to take decisive action. It came after they overheard a phone conversation between Ernani and his son, Marcello. They were going to Egypt. Flights were booked, tickets arranged. They were going to buy an apartment in Sharm al-Sheik, it seemed.

★ ★ ★

In May 2008 Ernani and Marcello arrived at Rome's Fiumicino airport. Commandante Zupo's men, supported by Rome police officers, pounced. The Barrettas were carrying 120,000 euros. There was nothing illegal in what they were doing, they protested. They were flying to Egypt to buy a house and the payment had to be in cash. Their protests were in vain. They were handcuffed and taken off to police headquarters in Rome.

'Go!'

The order was given to 80 police officers on 24 May. With police beacons flashing on their cars, they raced in through the gates of Rifugio Valle Grande, much to the astonishment of Ernani's staff, and swarmed all over the premises within seconds.

They dug up the gardens, delved into flower pots, the swimming pool and even looked for hollowed-out places in the towering Jesus statue beside the heli-pad. They tapped every wall for empty spaces and looked inside the hanging lanterns in the garden. They gained access to all the cars and searched them thoroughly, then seized them with the justification that they had been acquired with the proceeds of crime. Several of the men used metal detectors in case any stashes of cash were buried in metal containers, as they surmised might be true following one of Ernani's reference, in a phone conversation, to a tin can containing money.

They searched the wine cellar, stacked high with vintage bottles. Heavy crates of wine were shifted; the tools in a workshop were moved aside; the attic was torn apart. The search was painstaking, but it was undeniably thorough.

From on-high, the police moving around the land surrounding the country house of Ernani Barretta would probably have looked like worker ants going about their business – there were so many officers searching and digging that it seemed nothing could escape their eye.

Now and again a cry went up – an officer had found a bundle of euros – but it was mere piggy-bank money compared to the large amount that was missing. There *had* to be more stashed somewhere.

Then, came a breakthrough of sorts. During a search inside the house one of the officers delved into an empty decorated vase and pulled out pages containing sketches, arrows and notes that seemed to describe hiding places of some kind. It was a boy's own treasure map. Although it was intended to deceive the casual onlooker, police analysts were quickly able to work out where more large bundles of euros could be found. They headed towards rockeries and certain trees and added the discovered money to that which had already been found.

Some of the searchers paused to gaze at a photo on the wall showing Ernani shaking hands with none other than the German Chancellor, Angela Merkel. The officers were astonished – until they discovered later that the picture, like everything else, was fabrication; it was a clever Photoshop job, putting the German leader and the man who claimed to walk on water, in the same frame.

When the raid was finally over police were in possession of 1,650,000 euros. It was well short of the money that Helg Sgarbi had conned from his victims, it was true, but it was a start.

'*Even allowing for the money he's spent on villas and cars and what they were carrying at the airport, there has to be a substantial amount out there somewhere,*' prosecutor Gennaro Varone told Commandante Zupo. '*He'll either have to tell us – or somebody will – or we'll find it ourselves. We won't give up.*'

WHERE IS THE MONEY?

If the wives of Ernani and Helg thought they were safe from prosecution, they were mistaken. Police arrested them, too, as accomplices. Varone learned of other people linked to the group, but believed he did not have sufficient evidence to lay charges against them.

★ ★ ★

As the jail door banged shut behind him, pending what he now knew would be a court appearance and then a trial, Ernani began protesting his innocence ... The money that the police had found had been legitimately earned and hidden for security reasons; the houses and cars had been purchased with bank loans; he was with Helg Sgarbi in Germany, Switzerland and Austria because they were such old friends and often spent holidays together. In any case, he said, the money that the police said that they had found in his grounds was more than he had hidden and that meant only one thing – the police had planted it there to incriminate him. If Helg Sgarbi had taken money from Susanne Klatten, he insisted, it was in atonement for her family's Nazi history and his grandfather's horrible treatment by them. It was personal, he continued, between the Swiss man and the German woman and was nothing to do with him. He, Ernani Barretta, was just a hard-working businessman.

In the weeks that followed Ernani's arrest in May 2008, his lawyers issued a long diatribe against the police. He was an innocent man, they insisted. And Ernani was to repeat this over and over again as the days behind bars turned into weeks, and the weeks into months.

THE GIGOLO EXPRESSES REGRET

As a gesture of his faithfulness to God – or rather to God's Messenger on Earth, Ernani Barretta – Helg Sgarbi fixed a small cross to the wall of his cell in Munich's Stadelheim Prison. The confines of cell 310 in the west wing of the jail could not by any means be compared to the many luxurious hotel rooms that he had stayed in during his years of trawling Europe for rich and lonely women, longing for love and companionship. In his victims Helg, too, had found companionship of sorts, but now, apart from short breaks for exercise, he was alone in these very bleak quarters.

In an attempt to brighten up his surroundings, Helg also fixed images of mountain scenes and fields to the wall, images that he knew would be the only landscapes he would gaze at for some time to come. He knew they had him – his conviction seemed to be a 'done deal', as they say – but the question was whether he should put up a fight; suggest that the women had given him their money willingly. He had certainly not put a gun to their heads, after all. On the other hand, he knew the authorities had proof that he had sent threatening letters – those 'pay-up-or-else' missives – to his victims.

The prisoners who occupied nearby cells were given an insight, more so than any outsiders, into Helg's holistic attitude to life, for beside the food flap on the iron door was a sign declaring that he was a vegetarian and that the bread he was given should be brown.

Word had got around about his various, rather impressive female conquests and many prisoners saw in him someone to be admired. Some of them saw Helg as superior to his inmates. He hadn't engaged in armed robberies to gain huge bundles of cash; no, he'd actually talked those women into giving him millions of euros! This man, Helg Sgarbi, had actually had sex with all those women and then persuaded them to give him more cash than most crooks could ever dream of. *He was a genius!*

In the recreation areas, Helg mixed well with the other prisoners. They saw him as a polite, friendly man, who was at ease with everybody, even the most hardened of criminals, and he was able to hold a conversation with foreign inmates, for his knowledge of French, Italian and English broke down most communication barriers.

Some of Helg's inmates came to him to discuss their cases – they were waiting for their first court appearances or preparing an appeal – and it was in these discussions that his earlier legal training came into play. He was so prepared to help them that they began referring to him as the 'Gigolo Good Samaritan'.

He was always open and friendly but all he did was grin when asked about his extraordinary love life, particularly when quizzed by inmates about his conquest of heiress Susanne Klatten. However, it was no secret to those who were able to read the same newspapers and magazines that he pored over that kept track of what was being said about him in the outer world. He would cut out any articles that referred to him and store them in a cardboard shoe box in his cell. If he said anything about the heiress, it was merely to pass comment on the fact that she was a charming woman and he became annoyed if pressed for further gossip about her.

Of equal, understandable, fascination to his peers was what he had done with all the money.

'*I don't have it any more*,' he said – and his words seemed to ring true.

Others still wondered what it was that he had that they didn't. He did not look like a lady-killer, what with his spectacles, nondescript haircut and his rather precise way of speaking. He looked more like a bank clerk or a computer geek. Perhaps, they suggested among themselves, he was more well-endowed than any of them realized, but they weren't going to find that out when he took his twice-a-week communal shower: he modestly kept his underpants on as the water flowed down over his thin body.

★ ★ ★

The authorities wanted Helg to tell them where the money, and also where any copies of the sex videos and photos were. They wanted to hear him confess that it was all in the hands of Ernani Barretta, but Helg remained silent on that front, only repeating occasionally, as he had to his fellow prisoners, that he did not have any of it in his possession. He made no reference to Ernani at all, much to the frustration of his interrogators from the Landeskriminalamt and also the prosecutor's office.

His choice of lawyer had also come as a surprise, especially if even a glimmer of Ernani's claims, at the time of his own arrest, were true – that Helg had probably acted out of revenge for the Quandt family's use of slave labour from the concentration camps. Helg had employed 77-year-old Egon Geiss, a legal veteran who had made his name defending Nazis, to act in his defence.

Why had Helg brought him in? Perhaps, with his knowledge of Germany's dark Nazi past, the lawyer would argue convincingly that Susanne Klatten and the Quandt family did have something to answer for in the hope that it might besmirch her reputation.

The question of whether Susanne would be summoned to the witness box in Helg Sgarbi's trial was one on everyone's minds. Certainly, it would be the last thing that the publicity-shy heiress would want, for once she was there she would be forced to supply details about her affair and she might even be accused of leading him on.

Susanne would not be called to the stand, however, if Helg agreed to plead guilty to extortion and she would be spared further embarrassment. But if the prisoner took the 'not guilty' plea, it was certain that Susanne and, most probably, other victims as well, would be called to give evidence against him. If she expressed reluctance to do so, even if the judge sympathized with her, there was the threat that Geiss might invoke Paragraph 220 of the German Criminal Code, of which he was an expert, which gave him the right to overrule a judge and call his own witnesses.

These were the variables that State Prosecutors Christian Schmidt-Sommerfeld and Thomas Steinkraus-Koch considered as they prepared the case against Helg Sgarbi. Mr Schmidt-Sommerfeld was no stranger to sensational cases – just one year earlier he had issued arrest warrants for 13 suspected CIA agents over their alleged kidnapping in 2004 of a German national. The agents were said to have wrongfully imprisoned Khaled al-Masri and caused him serious bodily harm. Now the Munich prosecutor had another major case on his hands as he prepared fraud and blackmail charges against Helg Sgarbi. The same charges would be laid against him in relation to victims Susanne Klatten and three other women, who were to be identified for the record by initials only.

It had taken a great deal of persuasion to get statements from the other women, once they had been tracked down, but Susanne was more than willing to co-operate with the authorities. The team of prosecutors were filled with admiration at her courage because she had been warned that this rather sensational story was certain to leak out to the press and outer world. She was prepared for that, she said. As she had decided earlier, she was doing this not just for her own sake, but for all of the other women who had or might succumb to Helg Sgarbi and men like him in the future.

Senior police officials and adjudicators were not interested in putting Susanne through the ordeal of describing the sexual side of her relationship with Helg, but they were keen to know essential details of how she had come to be blackmailed: how Helg had first approached her, where the money had been exchanged, and the meaning of the '7-Up' code. Because of the international agreement enabling co-operation between police of different European countries, the German investigators could ask Susanne specific questions that might answer issues that the authorities in Switzerland, Austria and Italy might have with their cases.

Susanne provided dates and places of her meetings with Helg but what was of concern to the Swiss authorities was what she had been told about Helg's time in the armed forces of that country. She was asked to detail what he had said to her about his training and how he had leaked the information that he was a 'special adviser' in crisis areas. Even though there is no evidence that he was anything of the sort, the authorities were anxious to know just what he had told her and whether anything he had disclosed was of a sensitive nature, militarily. They also wanted to know if he had claimed to be attached to the Swiss Embassy, given that he had told her he had a diplomatic passport. Anyone professing to be an attaché, when they were not, could create chaos in diplomatic circles if they made such claims while abroad.

Of particular interest to the Italians was the role that Ernani Barretta had played during Susanne and Helg's affair. In her meetings with Helg – especially during her holiday in the South of France – had she noticed another person with Helg? Had she noticed the Italian man in the photograph with him? To both questions she shook her head. No, she said, she'd seen no-one like that and, in any case, Helg had assured her that they were very much alone, although she knew differently now from the photographs and recordings.

'*Does the name Ernani Barretta mean anything to you?*' she was asked. No, she replied, it does not.

During her question-and-answer session with the German authorities, Susanne raised the matter of the information Helg had received about her … How had he known that she had visited Egypt and Jordan, even down to the precise areas she had been to? Very few people knew that. How also was he aware that she was interested in renewable energies? She told them about the only person who knew of her travels – an academic she had often spoken to. The police made a note of his name, while accepting that if he had passed on information it might well have been unwittingly. Helg Sgarbi, they knew, was a cool, clever and convincing operator, skilled at uncovering information about his targets well before he moved in on them.

She also spoke of seeing a woman that she knew because their children attended the same school (identified as 'G' in this book), in the resort of Kitzbühel one day. She remembered seeing 'G' with a man who, on reflection, she believed was Helg Sgarbi. The couple, she said, appeared at the time to be very much in love – but that was before Helg Sgarbi had introduced himself to her at the Lanserhof.

The formal interviewing of the heiress was now over, but there was a woman in Italy who still pleaded with Susanne to be heard: Gabriele Sgarbi.

THE GIGOLO EXPRESSES REGRET

Under house arrest, her access to bank accounts frozen, she was left alone without the support of either her husband, or her guru and alleged lover, Ernani, to care for her two-year-old daughter. She wanted her husband back and there was only one hope, she said. It lay in the very woman that Helg had defrauded. She began writing to Susanne Klatten. Gabriele told Susanne that while she accepted that her husband had committed adultery with her, she was now writing out of desperation – woman to woman, mother to mother. Could Susanne really live with herself, knowing that Helg had a young daughter who was pining for him? Was it right that a child should grow up without a father in the years to come?

'*You have much influence in this case and I ask you to forgive him and allow him to have his freedom to see his daughter,*' she wrote. Gabriele went on to admit that her husband had made a huge, even inexcusable mistake, but even so she begged the heiress to show him some mercy. She pointed out that she had been just as violated by his adulterous actions as Susanne herself had been. It was his affair with Susanne that had led to the blackmail attempt, she wrote, a veiled suggestion that Susanne's involvement was partly to blame for Helg being in prison.

The letter ran to two pages. She slipped it into an envelope and asked Italian police to ensure that it reached Susanne before her husband appeared in court.

As the date approached for Helg to stand before a judge, news organizations across Europe ran wild with speculation. From the time it was learned that a man who had allegedly tried to blackmail the BMW heiress was sitting in a German prison, TV and radio stations, newspapers and magazines scraped together every detail about the saga.

Based on what poured out from every news organization in Europe Helg Sgarbi and Ernani Barretta had already been judged and convicted. They had been paired in a massive conspiracy to dupe and extort rich women and, if Helg, the first to appear in court, was convicted and sentenced to jail, it seemed that Ernani, his reported partner in crime, was equally doomed.

The Italian authorities, counting up the money and the value of Ernani's cars and properties alone, had already concluded that they had more than enough physical evidence to win a conviction against him, whatever happened to Helg.

But how were Helg and his lawyer really going to play it?

The heavy-jowelled, stern-faced and elderly Egon Geiss was a prominent figure in German legal circles and was known as 'The Fox' because he was so wily. Munich prosecutors went back over a number of his most famous cases to try to find clues as to how he might defend Helg Sgarbi in this case. What stood out, it seemed, was Geiss's clever use of Clause 220, which was to change the way many lawyers worked.

Geiss himself gave nothing away in the weeks leading up to Helg's court appearance. He was often to be found working late in his office and he preferred to make the more than 3-hour trip to visit Helg in prison by train rather than car as it gave him an opportunity to review the large number of documents that seemed to fill his briefcase.

Anton Winkler, speaking on behalf of the Munich prosecutor's office, got in the first shots in the days before Sgarbi's trial began by suggesting that Helg could expect some leniency if he were to plead guilty. '*If he makes a confession, if he spares his victims from having to appear here in public, he will get a corresponding reduction in his sentence,*' he said.

★ ★ ★

On the morning of Monday 9 March 2009, Helg Sgarbi was led handcuffed into the court. He was dressed in a three-piece grey suit that looked at least one size too big for him, a white shirt and a blue tie with green spots. His hair was neatly combed and he wore a pair of brown-framed spectacles. No-one looked less like a woman-swooning gigolo than the geeky figure that Helg Sgarbi presented. As one observer scornfully noted: '*If that's a gigolo, what do Swiss accountants look like?*' This was really the man who had seduced the richest woman in Germany? This was the object of her lust and that of several other women? There was not even a hint of that sad, little boy-lost countenance that had won Susanne Klatten over; there was just a thin man in a grey suit, wearing a smug grin as he peered around the courtroom to await the appearance of Judge Gilbert Wolf.

THE GIGOLO EXPRESSES REGRET

The moment finally came when the defendant was asked how he wanted to plead to the charges of fraud and attempted extortion. His reply would determine whether Susanne Klatten and the other alleged victims might be summoned to publicly recount their stories.

'Guilty', he said.

And so, it seemed it was over, virtually before it had begun. But there were still some formalities. Helg wished to make a brief comment.

'*I deeply regret what has happened and apologize to the aggrieved ladies in this public hearing,*' he said.

With those words, the Prosecution understood that he had pleaded guilty to save his victims the ordeal of being called to give evidence. But he declined to reveal where the money had gone, what had happened to the videos and with whom he had been working, if anyone.

Prosecutor Steinkraus-Koch asked the court to sentence Helg to nine years in jail. His lawyer, Mr Geiss suggested that a sentence of around five years was appropriate.

Judge Wolf leafed through Helg's curriculum vitae and read out an impressive reference from Credit Suisse. Describing the attempted extortions by using videos of intimate encounters as 'the gravest crime', he sentenced Helg to six years in jail. Helg opened his arms wide, in that gesture of his that would be familiar to Susanne and the other women who had crossed his path. This time the message was clearly: '*You got me*'.

After the so-called Swiss gigolo was led away to begin the coming years in the company of men, Judge Wolf commented that Helg's '*confession spared his victims from having to testify in court and thus saved them from further public exposure. That was very important to us.*'

The judge added that Helg was not likely to get any parole '*given that he still has the money and hasn't revealed anything about that.*' He was certain that Helg would serve his full-term.

As well as receiving a jail term, the court decreed that any of Helg's assets might be uncovered and frozen for three years to help his victims recover damages. That was if any assets could be found, particularly the money. Attention would now turn to the Italian authorities, who had found secret stashes of euros at Ernani's country estate …

Helg's lawyer had little to say after his client was led away. '*I'm content with the verdict,*' he said. '*It's pretty much in the range I had asked for. They could have sentenced him to 12 years or even 15.*'

Mr Steinkraus-Koch, however, insisted that the confession and a jail sentence that was much lower than he'd expected shouldn't be interpreted as being in Helg's favour. '*The confession does not include horses and riders,*' he said in a veiled reference to Helg's alleged controller, Ernani Barretta – who was yet to go on trial – and to anyone else who might have benefited from Helg's work as a money-making seducer. Anyone else who might be charged and convicted in the future could not expect clemency.

Anton Winkler, speaking for the prosecution, said that his colleagues would analyze the court's ruling before deciding whether to appeal against the sentence. One thing was clear in what he had to say next – that Helg Sgarbi was a master of his trade. '*He seems to have been quite charming. He was responsive to women,*' said Mr Winkler. And in a reference to those who were lonely and wealthy he added: '*He knows the problems that women like that have and it was therefore quite easy for him. I'd say he was a professional at this game.*'

During the trial, Susanne remained at home with her family, hoping and praying that she would not be called as a witness. The relief was enormous when she heard that the man who had so calculatingly allowed her to expose all her emotions to him was now behind bars.

Her father had warned her about the potential pitfalls of wealth, she had told a German newspaper shortly before the court hearing. He had instilled in her a sense of duty to be benevolent, but she had also learned to question the honesty of the people she met.

Immediately after the hearing, Susanne left it to her spokesman, Jörg Appelhans to comment. '*Once she realized the relationship with Mr Sgarbi was based on criminal intent to betray her and extort money, she was determined to take action,*' he said. '*She was fully aware that by pressing charges she would face the unpleasant consequences of opening her private life to public scrutiny.*'

In a brief reference to her ordeal, Susanne told German newspapers *Financial Times Deutschland* and *Bild* that '*It hurts ... one needs to have thick skin, which I don't have. I have to distance myself from it … [I] was right to go this way, even if it wasn't easy.'*

She added to the *Financial Times* that she had been moved by the letters of support that she had received since this had all come to light. *'From friends, colleagues, old classmates I haven't seen in 35 years. I'm very moved by it. It hurts that I've always been judged by my wealth … I'd just be happy to be finally treated like a normal human being.'*

While Mr Steinkraus-Koch praised Susanne for her courage in coming forward when other women victims were reluctant to do so, there was widespread speculation that her marriage was doomed. But friends close to the family said Jan Klatten was standing by Susanne.

★ ★ ★

Internet bloggers hit the keyboards with a wide variety of opinions as details of the extraordinary saga spread around the world. Some went right back in time to examine Susanne's family's links to the Nazis. One blogger identified as Bermanator, referring to the TV documentary that revealed the Quandt background, commented:

> *'Mrs Klatten has repeatedly demonstrated the Holocaust just "isn't her problem". What the program suggested is absolutely true – that her ancestors worked closely, manufacturing for Hitler during the war. Afterwards they grabbed up what was left of BMW – a company that had enslaved more than 10,000 Jews during the Holocaust … Her fortune is derived directly from the enslavement of Holocaust victims – she has flat out refused discussion of reparations to the victims of her wealth.'*

But a blogger identified as Babysnake summed up what many others were thinking: *'I applaud this courageous, if lonely and gullible woman.'*

While it seemed that the ordeal suffered by the BMW heiress was now over, Susanne knew that there would be more to come. For sitting in a cell in Italy was the man accused of masterminding the whole blackmail racket. It was he, police were convinced, who possessed Susanne's money. And who knew what he was going to reveal?

THE GURU PROTESTS
HIS INNOCENCE

Helg Sgarbi had no defence. While he had kept Susanne's correspondence to him in order to extort more money from her, she in turn had kept his – and she and the police had used it to convict him. Even if he had denied being the author of at least one blackmail letter, which accompanied the intimate photographs sent to the heiress, he had made the simple mistake of leaving his fingerprints and his DNA on them. It was as basic a mistake as Ernani Barretta overlooking the possibility that Italian police might be tapping his phone.

Unlike Helg, who, given the overwhelming evidence against him had put his hands up to the crime, Ernani was not going to make it easy for the investigators. As he was to repeat in his recorded phone conversations, Susanne Klatten was an incredibly powerful woman and he regretted being involved in the plan to target her but as a precaution had burned all documents and dumped all computer images relating to that plot. At least, he *thought* he had done so.

Following Ernani's arrest at Rome airport and the subsequent raid on the Rifugio Valle Grande, he had been held on a charge of laundering money from the proceeds of criminal activities and also on conspiring in an attempted blackmail plot. He had been denied bail. He was 63 years old at the time and he was determined not to live out the best of his remaining years behind bars. He would fight all the way.

He called in veteran lawyer Sabatino Ciprietti, who immediately began the task of defending '*an astute businessman who had earned every single euro honestly*'. Details of his defence came through Mr Ciprietti and Ernani's colleagues. It was totally untrue that all that money had been found at the Rifugio Valle Grande and so the question remained where the police had got it from. In any case, the money that the police had seized was for the most part in Swiss francs and there was only a small amount there in euros. That money, it was claimed, had not even been found at the complex because it was being kept at a property some 3.2km (2 miles) away.

Mr Ciprietti's comments were seen as attempting to distance Ernani from German-issued euros that could have been suspected as coming from the Klatten money passed to the Italian by Sgarbi. Although more money was found by police at a property some 2 miles away, they were able to raid it under their warrant because those premises are understood to have been owned by Ernani.

'To claim that money was scattered everywhere around Rifugio is quite ridiculous,' claimed Ernani's associates.

As for the assets, the cars and the homes, they had been held by the Barretta family for years and a simple check would prove that they had not been purchased with the proceeds of crime. The family had not only earned their money through business deals, but it had been supplemented by bank loans to develop Rifugio Valle Grande, which was a legitimate business. Over the years it had played host to over 10,000 people, who had gathered there for conferences, weddings, birthday celebrations and private dinners. Even respected politicians had met there and enjoyed the fine hospitality. The courts, said Ernani's people, had ample documentary evidence of the movement of money in relation to the family's business activities, including copies of contracts, cheque stubs and tax receipts.

Ernani was further incensed. They had absolutely no right to keep him in jail, he said, but his outpourings of anger made no difference. The months rolled by, the self-styled guru's alleged powers of being able to walk on water and transform himself into another being who could fly through space and end up in another place, seemingly ineffective at being able to lift him out of the grim surroundings of San Donato jail.

He knew that other inmates, trusted ones, were allowed out for 'work experience', but he was not among the chosen ones. He had also been made aware of the extraordinary amount of coverage the case of the gigolo, the heiress and the '7-Up' blackmail plot had generated around the world – linking him in almost all reports with Helg Sgarbi and describing him as the 'collector' of the money his 'disciple' was prising from his lovers.

He had also learned that he was alleged to have made a call, telling one of Helg's victims that it would be the worse for her – and for Helg – if she did not pay up. The implication being that the threat was from one of the men working for the US Mafia Don. Aware of that evidence, Ernani was preparing to issue a strong denial that he was the caller.

His lawyer, Mr Sabatino, was playing his part in trying to convince the world of his client's innocence and he agreed to give an interview to the German ZDF TV network in November 2008. Money that had been given to Ernani by women living at the country house had been done so freely. As for any involvement with the Klatten case, Mr Sabatino said there was no evidence that Ernani had anything to do with that. The money found on the Rifugio premises had been generated from the hotel and tourism and all of Ernani Barretta's assets could be accounted for legally. As for the allegations that Ernani Barretta had shot videos of Helg and Susanne, Mr Sabatino said that there was absolutely no evidence and his client was not even aware that Susanne Klatten was one of the richest women in the world.

It was put to the lawyer that behind the blackmail attempts lay a sect, of which Ernani Barretta was the leader.

He replied: '*There is no sect and there is no evidence.*'

Then came the important question as to what had happened to the money extorted from Susanne. '*It's not proven,*' said Mr Sabatino. '*It's just what Mrs Klatten says.*'

For his part, in that same month of November 2008, Ernani sent a letter to *Il Giornale* newspaper in which he denied being a cult guru and stating that he was worried about his reputation.

'*I hope that God helps me and that I finally succeed in demonstrating my innocence in this case,*' he wrote. He continued that he did not know Susanne Klatten; she did not know him and he had thousands of friends and clients who could speak up for him. He had, in fact, received more than 400 letters of support. He was no Don Giovanni, the insatiable lothario, neither was he a Rocco Siffredi, an Italian porn star. He added a reminder that Italian law stipulated that the accused was innocent until proven guilty – and that applied to him, all his friends and family.

As a protest against his continued confinement he began a hunger strike, taking in only water. It got him nowhere.

In late January 2009, Ernani Barretta stood before Judge Maria Gabriella Tascone in the Pescara Court. Ernani's lawyer asked for bail. The prosecution, however, said that even without copies of the many DVDs that had been made of Helg and Susanne, police were in possession of a wealth of evidence. Mr Ciprietti pressed home the appeal for bail. The judge shook her head. Aware of the alleged link between the Italian man and the Swiss gigolo, she knew that the result of the case against Helg Sgarbi had to be decided and, at the time, that was at actually at least two months away.

As further reasons for Ernani's continued incarceration, the judge cited the risk of escape and the possibility that evidence could be tampered with. She was also aware of the row that would erupt should the German authorities learn that Ernani had been allowed to walk from the court.

After five attempts to obtain bail, Ernani Barretta succeeded in winning his right to leave his prison on 21 February 2009 and return to Rifugio Ville Grande. As he stepped from the prison, his son, Marcello, who had been charged with being an accomplice but who was out on bail, was waiting for his father and wrapped his arms around him. Ernani looked a shadow of his former self; he seemed to have aged about 10 years. His previously dyed dark hair was now as grey as his sunken cheeks. Stubble adorned his face.

But he repeated what he had said earlier in his open letter to *Il Giornale* – that he did not know Susanne Klatten or any of the other women that Helg Sgarbi had seduced, but he was more than happy to invite them to his home and he would cook them a plate of spaghetti, even though they had 'massacred' him.

He was a good man, he insisted, a hard worker, having toiled in Germany and Switzerland, but in the end his heart had led him back to Pescosansonesco. He had saved many young people from the scourge of drugs. They had seen only goodness in him, which is why they had sought him out and he had given them his blessing and put them on the road to success.

Then he showed even more vanity: on 26 March he would be 64, not 68 years old as had been reported, but he carried no grief towards anyone. He wanted to reopen a pub he owned, *The Blockhouse*, which had been closed following his arrest, and then get down to writing a book about his life, detailing a history of hard work. '*It is a beautiful story that nobody else wants to tell, so it will be for me to tell it.*'

Two months later, with Helg beginning his long incarceration in Munich, Ernani was back in court. He was a new man, having put on weight and dyed his hair. In his immaculate dark suit, blue shirt, regimental striped tie and shiny brown shoes he had won back those 10 years. There was a soft smile on his face and he had a new lawyer, Carlo Taormina, who described the case as '*amusing*'.

Mr Taormina moved in high places, inside and outside the court rooms. A friend of Prime Minister Silvio Berlusconi, he had represented Mafia members and disgraced politicians. But he had also defended Nazi war criminal Erich Priebke, a former SS officer, who, in 1996, was convicted of participating in the massacre of 335 civilians at the Ardeatine caves in Rome in March 1944. Mr Taormina's other famous case was the defence of Anna Maria Franzoni, who in 2004, was sentenced to 30 years imprisonment for allegedly bludgeoning to death her three-year-old son in a family chalet in the Alpine village of Cogne.

Ernani Barretta, said Mr Taormina, was a blameless businessman who had sat in jail because '*a woman wanted to have sex with a man who my client is friends with.*'

Ernani had his say, too. He smiled as he claimed that '*only lies have been written about me. I am a respectable businessman. I run a hotel in which more than 19,000 guests have stayed and the money that the police found in my house are my savings. I don't trust any bank – but that is not a crime. My father told me not to put money in the bank but to bury it. The cash the police have dug up is the result of 40 years of hard work.*'

As for the claims that Susanne Klatten was no stranger to him, his lawyer said Ernani had never met her. '*My client never had her business card in his pocket. A piece of paper with telephone numbers was found in his car because someone had lost it there.'*

The hearing lasted just a few minutes before it was adjourned. Outside the court Mr Taormina was asked why his client was in the adjoining room to that of Helg Sgarbi and Susanne Klatten at the Holiday Inn.

'*That has to be proven first,*' said the lawyer.

But what of the money – where was it?

'*What money?*' asked Mr Taormina. '*My client only has what he has earned himself and Herr Sgarbi was given his 7.5 million euro by Mrs Klatten as a gift. The sum is therefore not relevant to the case.*'

All would be proven, he said, if Helg Sgarbi could be brought to Italy and appear before a court as a witness. '*He will finally deny the charges against my client.*'

Various charges of association with Ernani's alleged crimes were to be laid out against Helg's wife, Gabriele, Ernani's wife, Beatrice, and his 32-year-old son, Marcello, and 35-year-old daughter, Clelia. By now, prosecutor Gennaro Varone had also added the names of two others to the list – Prisca Furger, 35, and Sandra Fabbro, 43, both Swiss nationals and residents of Pescosansonesco. They were accused of registering two pieces of real estate near the village with money said to have been from Helg Sgarbi's crimes.

Helg was in jail and Ernani knew that he was potentially facing jail. Even if he had turned his eyes towards the tall Jesus statue towering above his residence, he may have wondered if the Lord would be able to perform a miracle to get him out of this mess.

INTO THE GURU'S LAIR

At 3.32 in the morning of 6 April 2009, Ernani Barretta was woken by a violent shaking of his home. He and a handful of others staying at Rifugio Valle Grande ran out into the garden as the earth trembled beneath them. The earthquake was centred around the mediaeval city of L'Aquila, some 60km (37 miles) to the west, bringing down buildings and killing almost 300 people. But thousands of other villagers in the central Abruzzo region were terrified that their homes would collapse in the 6.3 magnitude jolt, which was felt as far away as Rome, 90km (56 miles) away.

The residents of Rifugio Valle Grande turned their eyes to the towering mountain behind. If there was a landslide, that would be the end of the house – and them. But the trembling ceased and, unlike the devastating earthquakes that had torn apart the old village decades before, Pescosansonesco had escaped damage this time.

The road to Pescosansonesco – both the 'old' village and the new one, built a few minutes drive away – follows a tight route through the mountains some 40km (25 miles) to the west of the seaside town of Pescara – Ernani Barretta's playground as a youth. But he had come a long way since then.

The turn-off from the Pescara–Rome autostrasse winds through the town of Torre de Passeri, before the road begins to climb up towards Ernani's domain on this warm sunny Sunday morning. It is necessary to drop down through the gears to deal with the twisting hill.

The road passes the quaint old village of Castiglione a Casauria, balanced so precariously on the edge of a cliff, and then it continues upwards. Soon another village comes into sight, again teetering on a cliff edge – the old Pescosansonesco that was largely deserted after the earthquakes of 1917 and 1933. But there is life here now.

INTO THE GURU'S LAIR

The bells on the Santuario Beato Nunzio Sulprizio ring out across the valley and a group of old men in braces sit at a table in the shade across the road from the centre of activity – the bar Trasatti. They sip bitter espressos and watch the occasional car drive by; most vehicles are driven by tourists on their way to the most modern building for kilometres around, the sanctuary towering above them, its alabaster walls a brilliant white. In a few hours, the coaches will begin to arrive, bringing pilgrims looking for a blessing, just as they had come when Ernani Barretta was a boy.

It seems astonishing that a simple man, born just 2 km from here in the new village, can have touched the world of Susanne Klatten and learned more about her than any other person on earth apart from her husband and Helg Sgarbi, including her bedroom secrets.

Perhaps, despite his previous denials, he will say something now. Journalists from around the world have door-stepped him for days before finally packing up their gear, going away empty-handed. The chances of a word from, or even a glimpse of, Ernani Barretta, whose name is now known around the world, seem slim, however.

It is first-gear up the narrow road, lined with brilliant red poppies and other wildflowers, to the entrance to Rifugio Valle Grande. The metal gates are closed and locked and so is a small metal doorway to the right. The engraved brass plate disclosing the name of the property is obscured by a piece of paper inviting those wanting to know about opening times to call a telephone number. But there will be no visitors for some time to come.

It is an impressive home, judging from the view through the gates. It is as high above the village as possible, stamping Ernani's lofty, unofficial role as 'Prince of Pescosansonesco'. And, towering up behind it, dwarfing the property, is the mountain. If, as the police claimed, Ernani has hidden his ill-gotten gains in this region, the spoils could be anywhere. Spend as much as a day heading into the foothills, find a nook and hide the loot. It's as simple as that, if it's true.

There is movement up by the house, beyond the manicured lawn. A dark-haired woman walks across the outside porch. And then a man on a small scooter drives past the same area. From a distance he looks like Ernani. There is no response from several presses of the intercom button but there is little doubt that each and every caller to the estate is carefully scrutinized through the two video cameras that are aimed down from the gateway's stone pillars.

Now a man in a brown T-shirt is heading down the driveway, seemingly taking his time. He is a giant with a crewcut; his biceps bulge. His manner suggests that he will put up with no nonsense. He is asked if Rifugio is open for business. *No.* He has a German accent. His stare is filled with suspicion. It says go away and don't even think of arguing about it ...

There is no option but to return to the village. Ernani is incommunicado. A coffee in the *Bar Trasatti*. The old men stare. These are Ernani's people. Some are of his age; others are as old as his father might have been, were he alive. The barman, who appears to be the owner, serves the coffee and hurries to the rear. A second coffee is ordered. Then, shortly afterwards, shadows fill the doorway. It is the giant from Rifugio along with a group of men. *Among them, astonishingly, is Ernani Barretta.*

They shake hands across the bar with the owner, and then order a red-coloured drink all round – topped up with spumante. They all touch glasses. There are big smiles, more handshakes. A pat on the back. It appears to be a celebration – or is it a show?

The only published photographs of Ernani appear to have been a small shot of him in his lounge room, taken several years before, and pictures of him coming and going from court. It is time for a new photo in the street, given that all the signs – the turn-away from the country house and the group of men surrounding him – are that he is not prepared to talk. A good position from which to take a picture is across the road, near the old men. One of Ernani's men comes to the door, looks around – and holds his stare for just a second too long. They are wondering if the visitor is still around ...

Then, they are all leaving the bar and Ernani is hidden from view, but they come across the road and in an instant the man himself is a foot away to the right and the German is to the left. The questions begin ... '*Who are you? What are you doing here? You are driving a car with*

INTO THE GURU'S LAIR

Swiss plates − are you Swiss?'

It is explained the car has been rented in Zurich but then the German is speaking rapidly in his native tongue, his raised hand indicating that there can be no protests that he is not being understood. Eventually satisfied, he breaks into English. Swiss journalists, German journalists, French journalists − none of them are welcome here.

They are truthfully, in return, told that a book is being written and that it's important that Ernani is spoken to, even though he does not speak English.

Many minutes pass as the two men, with interjections by the others, hold a discussion in Italian before an astonishing agreement is reached. Ernani will be available at the Rifugio in three hours time. First, he has an appointment in Pescara and then he will be happy to talk … perhaps. If he does, it will be for the first time, the visitor muses.

At the appointed time, though, the gates remain closed. There is no response from the intercom. There is no movement in the grounds. Half an hour passes; then an hour.

Up the hill two donkeys stand in the shade in a field of fruit trees. Beside the field is the Rifugio Valle Grande helicopter pad with the big letter 'H' and at the far end the looming statue of Jesus. The police have looked at it carefully for any sign of hidden money, although that would be perhaps a little too obvious. The mountain, that towering mountain, could take 100 years to scour … a much better option.

Finally a car comes up the hill. A woman in her 40s with a soft smile indicates she does not speak English, but she still manages to convey a message. Ernani is running late. Three more hours and he'll be back. She has the time of his expected arrival written on a piece of paper.

The light is fading as the revised time approaches. But there is a good sign that the group have finally returned − the German is walking down the hill above the country house towing one of the donkeys, the other walking freely behind.

Against an alleged background of grand theft and international blackmail, a burly German henchman walking the donkeys in the mountains of Italy seems bizarre. He leads the donkey into a field nearer the residence and then he opens the gates by remote control. They slowly swing open.

'*Come through,*' he says. '*You'll be the first.*'

The German makes conversation about the earthquake on the way along the curved tiled driveway to the house. '*Yes, everyone was frightened. Everything shook. People in the village ran from their houses.*' He looks up at the mountain. He doesn't have to say what he is thinking. If any of that came down ... '*It was a bad time but luckily there was little or no damage anywhere around here. But it shows how dangerous it can be living in these areas.*'

There is a children's playground on the grass, along with modern sculptures in white stone and some grottoes – and just in front of the porch is a fountain, circled by a low stone wall, with a lion-like figure standing in the water. It is familiar territory for the many hundreds of guests who have attended conferences and business lunches here, but now, since the police raid and the closing down of the business, it is a unique glimpse at Ernani Barretta's domain.

The German gestures to a table on the porch and then the woman who passed the message earlier to the visitor appears. In the few hours she has been away, she has learned to speak English well, it seems. Ernani will be out in a moment, she explains. She is a woman with a pleasant manner, although her actual relationship to Ernani remains a mystery.

The air is filled with fragrance from the flowers and shrubs. Bees buzz around the bright, yellow flowers in terracotta pots. A Perspex roof over the tiled porch allows the late afternoon light through and there is a rolled up blind for use in the height of summer. He will not be long, she says again.

And then there he is at the table. He has changed his shirt, from a t-shirt to a white collarless number since the morning, but he is still in the striped brown trousers and the beige running shoes. He wears a gold watch and two gold rings adorn the second finger of his left hand. There is a brown tint to his hair and an anxiousness to his manner, as if he is now questioning his decision to allow a stranger onto his property when so many others have been turned away.

With the assistance of his woman friend – or relative – he curses those who have written such *'bad things'* about him, in particular a particular Swiss journalist who has led the *'brigade of assassins'*.

'Bastardo! Bastardo!' he cries.

'They have crucified him,' says the woman. *'Ernani is a charismatic figure and those who want to destroy him have taken advantage of this, suggesting that he has another side to him, a bad side. As a result of these cruel things, his business has been closed down – and for what reason? Just because he knows this man, Helg Sgarbi, as an old friend, he has been joined in with him in this terrible affair.'*

It is clear that Ernani Barretta is going to make no confessions this evening. There will be no revelations about blackmail plots or bedroom scenes involving Susanne Klatten. The German sits in on the conversation as Ernani, assisted by the woman, tells his story. Sometimes he rises from the table to pace around the porch and the edge of the lawn as he insists he is a good citizen.

'Am I a victim or an executioner?' he asks. *'Everybody in the Abruzzo region knows me for who I am – a good businessman who has worked his way up from nowhere. I have been on TV and taken part in economical and political discussions so you can imagine how shocked people who really know me have been about this whole affair.'*

He is reminded of the claims that he filmed Susanne and Helg together, in particular the bedroom scenes in Munich's Holiday Inn.

'Yes, of course,' he says and the sarcasm and fury in his voice is unmistakable. *'I used a Black and Decker drill to punch a hole in the hotel wall and stick a camera lens through it. I drilled a big enough hole to be able to film the whole room and the bed and yet Susanne didn't see the hole and the hotel hasn't noticed it to this day. People who are suggesting I did that are just stupid.*

'If you want to film somebody who isn't supposed to be with you, you don't need an assistant and a camera and a Black and Decker drill. You can take a quick clip with one of these – ' and he picks up his mobile phone and waves it about. *'A clip on one of these would be enough … to prove an affair. She*

wouldn't even know you were doing it. You just pretend to be making a call, or answering one. You don't need a full-length movie, but that is what they're trying to claim and they're trying to claim it was me who made it. I'm furious about it: it's disgraceful.'

And Helg Sgarbi? … What of his relationship with Helg and the fact that they were found together in the car park at Vomp, when Susanne was due to hand over the fortune?

'He has been a friend for a very long time. We had a rapport from the beginning. We are spiritual people and we understand one another. There is no crime in that. When we first met in Europe, there was something we both recognized in each other that you cannot put into simple words. We knew we were of the same kind, that we had an inner understanding that others would not be able to comprehend.'

Ernani would not be drawn further on his relationship with the man who had seduced Susanne Klatten. He wanted the world to understand, however, that the money that had been used to build his country house was earned honestly through his own hard work.

'I was one of many children from a very poor background and I made up my mind from a very young age that I would not remain in the village to struggle for the rest of my life. I love this place, though, and my plan was to go out into the world, make good and return to the village and share my good fortune with others.

'I moved to Rome and worked there as a car mechanic and learned all the skills of the trade. When I travelled to Switzerland I bought and sold cars and began making enough money to start creating my own small empire. I just kept working my way up, buying and selling houses and making a good profit. This is where my money came from, not through any form of crime. I began buying classic cars, too, and they became the envy of many people. Old cars with style have been one of the great loves of my life.

'I bought this land, 30 hectares, when I returned to my beloved village and all my family helped to bring it to what it is today. We cleared all the trees, poured cement, brought the tiles and the stones up the mountain and began to build Rifugio Valle Grande. I made many sacrifices to bring this about. I could have enjoyed a more relaxed life, but I spent many years of hard work to create this beautiful place.'

He sweeps his arm around as if trying to embrace the huge property. *'Just look at it now – fruit trees, a restaurant for 300 people, a heliport. Visitors here can relax in the sunshine or go for mountain bike rides, perhaps. There is something here for everyone and it was all achieved through hard work, nothing else. This is what I do. Buy and sell. There was a house built in 1200 that I restored so that it could be used for bed-and-breakfast guests. It's my business and it is a good, clean business and the people who have come here – political people, church people, musicians, actors – they will all testify that it is one of the most perfect places in the whole of Italy.'*

But what of the claims that he ran a sect, virtually forcing his followers to work without pay, sleeping with the women and giving them back nothing apart from his blessing?

Ernani bangs his fist onto the table, his face red. *'Liars! Bastardoes! They have crucified me. People who say they have stayed here, who worked for me, have made it up. I have never heard of these people. They were never here. Why do they lie? Is it to make money?'*

He stands up. He has had enough of defending himself, he says. He wants his visitor to leave – *but wait!* One more thing. A tour of the country house, perhaps?

'You are privileged. Since these troubles no-one has been in here. I do not allow it. I will not allow spies or anyone who is going to speak out against me to come here. You must write the truth about me. Write these things that I have told you.'

A suit of shiny armour stands inside the main door, a hand extended to greet guests. Ernani, accompanied by the German and the woman interpreter who couldn't, but then suddenly could speak English, lead the way towards a small dining area.

On a wall on the left are photographs of Ernani's VIP guests, his face among those of the smiling visitors. There is a signed photograph by Bud Spencer, the Italian actor, filmmaker and former champion swimmer, who was born under the name of Carlo Pedersoli, and who continues to have a large fanbase throughout Europe. Then there is a photo of another high profile person Ernani says has been among his appreciative guests – Alessandra Mussolini, the blonde granddaughter of the former Fascist dictator Benito Mussolini. There is one more photo – the same 'posed' portrait that astonished police when they raided the property, Ernani shaking hands with German chancellor Angela Merkel. Raiding officers claimed that it was a 'Photoshop job', a digitally-manipulated merging of hands. There is certainly something unreal about the framed photo, which occupies pride of place on the wall among the many others, but Ernani does not allow a closer inspection.

He leads the way past a handful of round tables in the intimate dining area and into a vast hall with a long table set for 200 or so, wine glasses polished, plates and cutlery laid for guests who are unlikely to dine here for a long time to come. But there is more, for the dining hall is L-shaped and there is an equally long table in the second section, again with a table setting that is sadly lacking diners. The overhead lights are off and there is a feeling of gloom about the whole place.

'*When will they be back, your guests?*' Ernani is asked, although the answer that comes is to be expected. He shrugs, opens his hands.

'*He is hoping it won't be long,*' says the pleasant lady interpreter. '*He hasn't done anything wrong and it is terrible that he has been put out of business for this long time just because he knows somebody. He's very confident that his innocence will be proven and his good name and reputation will be restored.*'

Darkness is now falling. He has work to do, he says. He proffers a hand to the visitor. The German then leads the way back to the main gate.

'*Goodbye,*' he says, with just the hint of a smile.

The gates swing closed, locking Ernani Barretta inside his refuge. Only time would tell whether the wrought ironwork would be the only metal barrier he would be looking out through in the months to come.

EPILOGUE

It was *not* over.

Less than three months after Helg Sgarbi was sent to prison in March 2009, it was revealed that a new blackmail attempt had been made against Susanne Klatten. A man claimed to have a sex video of her, taken at the Holiday Inn during her liaison with Sgarbi. Unless she paid 75,000 euros for it, he claimed, it would be made public.

Mr Anton Winkler, the spokesman for the prosecutor's office in Munich, confirmed that there had been a copy-cat attempt to extort money from the wealthy BMW boss but, like Sgarbi before him, the unnamed blackmailer had ended up in the arms of the law.

When he contacted Susanne the man claimed that he had sex videos showing her in what he described as 'dangerous situations', but Mr Winkler said the man had neither sex videos nor any previous or existing relationship with Susanne.

As she went about picking up the pieces of her domestic life and threw herself into her corporate duties – preparing, among other events, for the annual shareholders meeting of her company Altana, AG – Susanne Klatten's lawyers began civil proceedings against Ernani Barretta in the hope of retrieving some of the millions.

The state of Susanne's relationship with husband Jan has not been commented on, but sources close to the secretive family suggest that the question of divorce had never been discussed.

Meanwhile, during a visit to Pescara, in which I met Ernani Barretta, he insisted that he did not have Susanne's money. That she would have to ask Helg Sgarbi where it was. However, Ernani added, he suspected that Sgarbi had lost it to the casinos.

He agreed that Helg was his 'best friend' and claimed that the Swiss man had told him that he had truly fallen in love with Susanne and wanted to take her to America with him.

'*All his other conquests were old and frustrated,*' Ernani declared as the countdown continued towards his own trial, '*… Susanne was younger, blonde and more successful than any of them. In the end, though, her beauty and her power proved to be his downfall. Along the way, she betrayed her husband and her family but I am determined she will not destroy mine or my reputation. One of us will prove to be the stronger.*'

PUBLISHER'S NOTE

At the time of publication in 2009, the publisher would like to make clear that Ernani Barretta still awaited trial.

Disclaimer
The description of events and interactions in this book are the product of the author's interpretation and dramatization of information provided to him via public records, media reports and interviews. The author has drawn his own conclusions in regard to such information and whilst these might be regarded by the reader as representing, in all instances, the factual recordal of events, they are not, and should not be interpreted as such.

AUTHOR'S NOTE

Research for this book took me on a 3,000km journey through Europe, seeking people who had been involved in the extraordinary story of the gigolo and the heiress. In some cases good fortune was on my side. For example, I happened to walk into a café in Uznach, Switzerland, and found that the only customer at the time was a woman who had just returned from her holidays but who had had a disturbing encounter with Helg Sgarbi while he was living in the town. Although she was not happy to give me her surname, she provided a number of details about the man who had once lived in a one-roomed apartment a little further up the street. On another occasion, in Italy, I was fortunate enough to become the first writer, at his personal invitation, to enter the sprawling mountain domain of Ernani Barretta – the man alleged to be Helg Sgarbi's partner in crime – since the police raid on his premises. He even showed me around and posed for a photograph.

But there were times when the shutters were down, as might be expected in a case such as this when one of the most secretive women in Europe – and one of the world's wealthiest – has been the victim of a crime that exposed a flaw in her life. For she admitted to investigators that she had 'strayed', although in her words she described her affair with Helg Sgarbi as a 'relationship'.

Exactly what occurred between them in their private moments together has never been revealed, for it is only Mrs Klatten or Helg Sgarbi who would be able to disclose that. Her code of silence means she is unlikely to ever 'kiss and tell' and Sgarbi has, for the time being at least, maintained his silence out of what he has told a court is 'respect for the ladies involved'.

The third alleged player in the gigolo–blackmail sting, the charismatic Italian Ernani Barretta, has denied being involved in a plot to blackmail the wealthy women of Europe, in particular Mrs Klatten. At least three of Sgarbi's 'conquests' have reluctantly given statements to police confirming they had affairs with him and paid him money, especially after he had applied pressure on them. There are suggestions from former associates of Sgarbi – who declined to reveal their identities – that there were other women in his life who paid money to him, either freely or under duress.

In the case of Mrs Klatten, I learned from the only publicly available legal document something of her relationship with Sgarbi – how they met, how she was persuaded to hand over millions of euros to him, freely at first, before he attempted to blackmail her with threats to expose their sexual liaisons to her husband and the board of BMW. In an interview with German authorities, she told of her first meeting with Sgarbi and how it continued on to a relationship. For the purposes of the story, I have reconstructed the conversations that passed between them, based very closely on the details she provided to investigators.

Details provided anonymously by associates of Helg Sgarbi and Ernani Barretta, along with comments by former associates of Barretta who have spoken to European publications in respect of any relationship between the two men and the operation of a sect, have also been built into the story based on my interpretation of the descriptions provided by those associates. All material in the book relating to Sgarbi's association with Barretta and Barretta's operation of a sect represents my own construction of the information imparted to me (and which I have no reason to question), and must be judged by the reader against Barretta's ongoing denial of any criminal association with Sgarbi and the existence of a sect. Although there are claims from Sgarbi's associates that a sect did exist, allegations that were published in newspapers in Europe, Barretta insists that was not the case, and he continued to deny it when I met him face to face.

In other areas of the book, I have attempted to follow Sgarbi's trail through Europe, visiting the Zurich University he attended, the town of Uznach where he lived, the sprawling luxurious hotel complex in Bad Ragaz where he seduced one of his victims and sitting in the lounge of the Lanserhof Spa where Sgarbi made his move on Mrs Klatten. Leaving no stone unturned, I also tracked down the autobahn restaurant and car park where Sgarbi hoped to receive his biggest-ever pay-off. As was often the case in my inquiries, the management refused to confirm that it was this car park where Sgarbi's scams came to an end, but persistent checks later gave me the confirmation I needed.

This story, then, taking into consideration the reference above to Barretta, is based entirely on fact, presented in a readable way. It is the stuff of novels – but it really happened. A self-confessed con man who now sits behind bars in Germany is testimony to that.

As for Ernani Barretta, he was still to come to trial at the time of publication, when he was continuing to deny being involved in extortion. It would be impossible to tell the story of Susanne Klatten and the gigolo without naming Ernani Barretta and time would tell whether he would walk free or end up behind bars like Sgarbi.

Richard Shears,
August 2009.

Helg Sgarbi:

Square-jawed, smooth-talking Gigolo and convicted blackmailer of BMW heiress Susanne Klatten. Born in Zurich in 1965 but spent his early years in Rio de Janeiro when his engineering father moved there. He returned to Switzerland for his teenage studies where he had a string of girlfriends, many of them from wealthy families. Originally had the surname Russak but on marrying a Swiss woman changed his surname to Sgarbi, his wife's maiden name.

Described by police as a smooth operator who knew how to win the trust of his victims. Claimed to be a 'secret agent' working for the Swiss government – a fake background that initially attracted his victims, before he poured out a make-believe story that the Mafia were after him because he had seriously injured the child of a Don in a car accident and he needed money as a pay-out.

Described as a specialist in mergers and acquisitions in a glowing job reference from Credit Suisse, read out in court before he was sentenced to six years jail for blackmail. First reported to the police in 2001 by 83-year-old Comtesse Verena Grafin du Pasquier-Geubels, who had given him several million euros.

Susanne Klatten:

Born Susanne Hanna Ursula Quandt in Bad Homburg, near Frankfurt, on 28 April 1962. Blonde and attractive, she is the richest woman in Germany and, with wealth estimated to be around £7 billion, she has been ranked by *Forbes* magazine as the 35th richest person in the world.

She owns a major part of BMW and the chemicals giant Altana. Her family – her late father, Herbert, mother Johanna and younger brother brother, Stefan Quandt – has been haunted by claims that their fortune comes from the Nazi regime, when Susanne's grandfather, Günther Quandt, owned factories that made batteries for Hitler's submarines.

Ernani Barretta:

Born in March 1945 in Pescosansonesco, Abruzzi, Italy. A swarthy, charismatic host of European VIPs at his mountain restaurant shortly before his arrest, Barretta is the alleged beneficiary of Helg Sgarbi's blackmailing plots. One of 10 children from a poverty-stricken family he earned his first pocket money as a boy showing tourists around the holy site of the Blessed Nunzio Sulprizio. Later trained as a stonemason and a car mechanic. Travelled to Rome to seek work before moving to Zurich, the home of his wife's mother. Set up business as a car salesman and later began to promote himself as a man who was blessed by the Holy Spirit. Promoted himself as a healer and enticed followers to donate money to his holy centre in his Italian village, to which he had returned. Later, it was alleged his finances were boosted by the gigolo earnings and blackmailing tactics of Helg Sgarbi. Charged with money laundering, court hearings against him continue in Italy, with police saying they have a watertight case proving blackmailing links to Helg Sgarbi.

Comtesse Verena Grafin du Pasquier-Geubels:

Born in Switzerland in 1918. Widowed after three marriages during which she obtained a title from a previous husband. She had spent most of her latter years living in luxury in the Hotel de Paris in Monte Carlo, but travelled at times to her villa on the shores of Lake Geneva.

She came into prominence when Sgarbi extracted $2 million from her after telling her a tale of woe – followed by her signing over to him nearly $30 million more. She became the first victim to go to the police and although much of the money was recovered, she was so infatuated with Sgarbi that she withdrew her complaint – leaving him free to continue hunting for other rich and gullible women.

CHRONOLOGY

1965 Helg Sgarbi is born as Helg Russak in Zurich, Switzerland. Later travels with his parents to Rio de Janeiro, Brazil, where he spends his early childhood, along with a younger sister. Continues his teenage education back in Switzerland and attends university in Zurich, where he studies law, before being drafted into the Swiss army. Eventually dismissed from the military as unfit for service on medical grounds and settles into life as an investment banker.

1994 Aged 29, Russak marries a Swiss girl but after two years they separate. Attends parties, has a string of girlfriends and in Zurich meets charismatic Italian Ernani Barretta, a car salesman.

2000 Russak and Barretta strike up a close friendship, with Russak remaining a faithful follower of Barretta's self-styled religious cult. Russak works with Barretta enlisting followers, and using his charms to entice young women into the flock. They donate large sums of money to Barretta's cult. Russak and Barretta begin plotting to extort millions of euros from gullible rich women.

2001 Russak is engaged to a cult member, Gabriele Sgarbi, and he uses her name as he sets about extorting money from wealthy women. In effect, he has become a gigolo. His first victim is a wealthy Englishwoman living in the south of France, but he soon targets Comtesse Verena Grafin du Pasquier-Geubels. He signs himself into Monte Carlo's opulent Hotel de Paris as Helg Russak and begins an affair with the 83-year-old widow. He tells her that the Mafia are after him for millions of dollars because he has seriously injured the child of a Mafia Don in the United States. She gives Russak the money in the belief they are soon to be married but he runs off and marries Gabriele instead. The Comtesse brings charges against him, then drops them and Russak-Sgarbi is free to continue his scams.

2002   Russak is now officially known as Sgarbi. He traps other wealthy women in his net but Ernani Barretta is allegedly providing the back-up: shooting videos and making recordings of Sgarbi with his victims whose affairs are threatened with exposure if they fail to hand over millions of euros.

2005   Sgarbi continues to prowl the mountain spa resorts, where wealthy women retreat. His story of the Mafia Don works on most occasions, although there are some women who brush him aside.

2007   Sgarbi and Barretta target Susanne Klatten, the richest woman in Germany and the 35th wealthiest woman in the world. Aged 45, she has been married for 18 years and is a mother of three. She has lived under a tight security net for most of her life and has been warned that her enormous wealth will always make her a target for con artists. Sgarbi tells Barretta that he also has a personal reason for targeting her – his Polish–Jewish grandfather suffered in her grandfather's wartime factories and this would be his revenge.

2007–08   Sgarbi moves in on Susanne at an Austrian health resort, the Lanserhof, and later they begin an affair. Sgarbi, once again, uses the Mafia Don story and Susanne hands over an initial 7 million euros to him. A recording of their love-making, secretly made with hidden cameras, is now in the hands of Barretta. Susanne begins to worry about Sgarbi's intentions but is then confronted by a new crisis – a documentary revealing her family's links to her grandfather's Nazi-associated factories. Sgarbi asks her to invest 290 million euros in the money markets and she ends their relationship. He sends her a sex video and demands 49 million euros as a pay-off. Susanne goes to the police.

2008   January: Sgarbi and Barretta drive to an autobahn rest-stop in Austria, expecting Susanne to arrive with a payment of 14 million euros, but the police arrest Sgarbi instead. Barretta is allowed to return to Italy where the Italian authorities are asked to begin proceedings against him.

2009   9 March: Sgarbi pleads guilty to charges of fraud and attempted extortion and is sentenced to six years in jail. The judge says he is unlikely to receive parole, given that he has not revealed the whereabouts of the large amounts of money cheated from his victims.

2009   May: Ernani Barretta and his son, Marcello, are arrested at Rome airport carrying 120,000 euros. Lengthy court proceedings begin against Barretta, in Italy, as he protests that his assets have all been bought legitimately.

ACKNOWLEDGEMENTS

The author is grateful to a number of individuals he met while reconstructing the events leading up to the blackmail of Susanne Klatten. Many of those contacted in Switzerland and Austria preferred to speak anonymously, among them witnesses to the arrest of Helg Sgarbi, but their assistance is acknowledged. While he denied involvement in crime with Helg Sgarbi, the interview with Ernani Barretta is also acknowledged.

Background material was drawn from a number of sources throughout Europe including:

(In Germany): *Der Spiegel, Bild, Die Welt, Financial Times Deutschland, Focus, Stern, Frankfurter Allgemein*

(In Switzerland): *Blick, Der Tages Anzeiger, Der Bund*

(In Italy): *Il Centro, Il Tempo, Il Giornale, Europa.*

(In UK): *The Times, Daily Mail, Independent, Daily Telegraph.*